To RAY

Love SANDY
7/11

Recipes from Historic

NEW ENGLAND

Other Books by the Authors

Recipes from Historic California

Recipes from Historic Colorado

Recipes from Historic America

Recipes from Historic Louisiana

Recipes from Historic Texas

The Great American Sampler Cookbook

At Ease in the White House

The New American Sampler Cookbook

How to Sell to the United States Government

The American Sampler Cookbook

The Homeschool Handbook

Recipes from Historic

NEW

ENGLAND

A Restaurant Guide and Cookbook

LINDA & STEVE BAUER

Taylor Trade Publishing
Lanham • New York • Boulder • Toronto • Plymouth, UK

Published by Taylor Trade Publishing
An imprint of The Rowman & Littlefield Publishing Group, Inc.
4501 Forbes Boulevard, Suite 200, Lanham, Maryland 20706
http://www.rlpgtrade.com

Estover Road, Plymouth PL6 7PY, United Kingdom

Distributed by National Book Network

British Library Cataloguing in Publication Information Available

Library of Congress Cataloging-in-Publication Data
Bauer, Linda.
  Recipes from historic New England : a restaurant guide and cookbook / Linda and Steve Bauer.
     p. cm.
  Includes index.
  ISBN 978-1-58979-439-9 (cloth : alk. paper) — ISBN 978-1-58979-440-5 (electronic)
  1. Cookery, American—New England style. 2. Restaurants—New England—Guidebooks. 3. Historic buildings—New England—Guidebooks. I. Bauer, Steve, 1943– II. Title.
  TX715.2.N48B38 2009
  641.5974—dc22   2009013707

∞™ The paper used in this publication meets the minimum requirements of American National Standard for Information Sciences—Permanence of Paper for Printed Library Materials, ANSI/NISO Z39.48-1992.

Printed in the United States of America

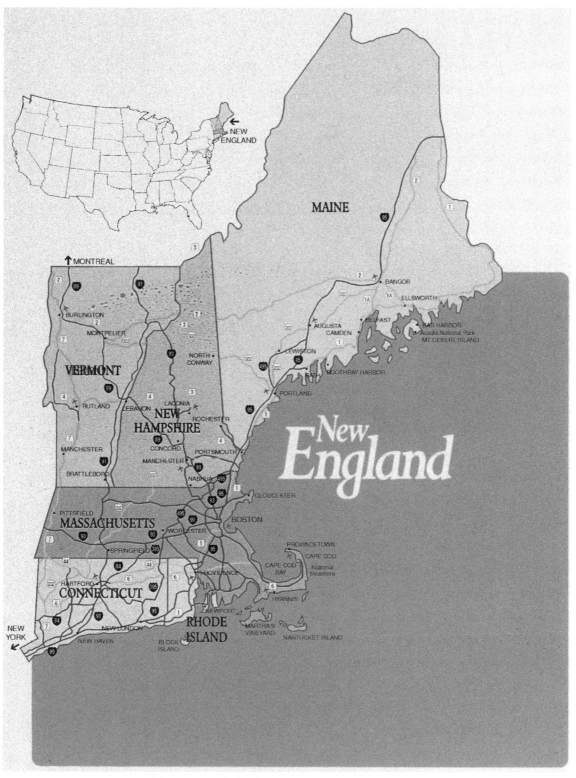

Map of New England. Source: *Discover New England.*

CONTENTS

INTRODUCTION

Recipes from Historic New England points the way to some of America's most historic and delicious establishments. They are full of flavor, fun, and storied pasts. Enchantment lingers with every mention of New England, the cradle of our republic. It is one of the finest places for families and friends who want to walk in the paths of our founding fathers from Boston to the Green Mountains to Old Sturbridge Village. Friendly and carefree New Englanders enjoy pubs, famous old breweries, a fine dinner train, and many family-run businesses to which diners come back for more.

The many varied types of terrain, ranging from mountains, beaches, forests, huge cities, and rolling hills to lakes and streams, provide breathtaking settings for dining and reliving the past. The climates along the coasts and valleys of America offer plenty of ways to work up an appetite from kayaking off the coast of Maine to mountain climbing in Vermont to skiing in New Hampshire to hiking in Massachusetts to sailing in Connecticut to running in Rhode Island. Tourists and natives alike enjoy all that the gorgeous region named New England has to offer. These historic venues and varieties of the freshest of local foods are healthy ways to serve up pride and preserve the past. Whether it is mixed greens on the golf course or in the salad bowl, New England is known for plenty of excellent outdoor activities and fresh and lively foods.

New England boasts countless travel and tourism destinations with food, entertainment, and sports for all ages and interests. The area is a paradise for the traveler, with history buffs enjoying the vast array of sites from homes to hotels, from seascapes to covered bridges to forested parks.

History has played a large part in the region's interest as seen through the mists of time. The chefs have worked together to form a variety of cuisines using the freshest of ingredients. New England cuisine is world famous.

In our more than twenty years of writing international food and travel columns, we have been amazed by the way an excellent restaurant with a special atmosphere enhances any dining experience or vacation. The combination of a historic venue and interesting cuisine, whether it is New England, Irish, French, Italian, American classic, or family style, makes for a fabulous dining adventure. It is exciting to enjoy a great meal in a former theater, bank, or historic hotel or at an old stagecoach stop.

Simply choose one of the regions and decide which historic restaurants profiled in this book to visit. Each restaurant is described with a page or more of history. The location and contact information are provided, along with several recipes that are served on the menu.

After a visit, the diner may wish to recreate the dish at home. Our experience has shown that many people love to read cookbooks and travel guides. This book offers both pleasures and allows singles, couples, and families to learn a great deal of about New England's history and enjoy its bounty of fresh produce, livestock, and excellent chefs.

Most of the restaurants are in the moderate price range, but they do vary. We have attempted to include all types. If cost is a factor, please phone for the price.

Remember: many of the restaurants in *Recipes from Historic New England* are very popular, and it is important to call ahead for reservations!

Bon appétit!

If you wish to have us speak at an event or fund-raiser, please contact bauerbooks@gmail.com or call (281) 292-6526. As we work our way down the East Coast, become a part of our journey. Please let us know if you have a favorite restaurant in a historic building. Thanks!

Massachusetts

BLANTYRE
Lenox

The nineteenth century saw the Lenox area expand with many great estates. At the time Lenox was already known as "the queen of inland resorts" or, as Cleveland Amory wrote, "the Switzerland of America." A prominent member of the summer community in the 1890s was John Sloane, a founder of the furniture store W&J Sloane. When he invited his friend Robert Paterson to Lenox, it was love at first sight. Paterson was completely infatuated with the area and its elegant way of life.

Paterson decided this was where he wanted to spend every summer with his wife, the love of his life, and his family. He acquired the 220-acre estate next door to Sloane known as "Highlawn" from the Dorr family so that he could build his dream house. It would be a spectacular property, built on a grand scale, although the architect's initial plans were allegedly drawn on the back of an envelope.

Paterson's concept was for no less than a castle of "feudal architectural features," complete with turrets and gargoyles. The house was modeled after his mother's ancestral home in Lanarkshire, Scotland. Construction began in 1901, at times employing more than three hundred people on the grounds and buildings. Besides the main house, there were seven outbuildings, such as an icehouse, stables for up to sixteen horses, and a carriage house, as well as extensive greenhouses.

Paterson's main house was furnished in the English style, with all the furniture being brought from England. Throughout there were beautiful pieces from the Paterson's extensive art collection. The featured painting in the Music Room is one of Henry Clive, painted by John Opie.

The Paterson family used the house every summer, entertaining frequently, as was the custom then. In a testament to the Gilded Age, they held garden parties with musicians imported from New York and grand dinner dances, with each event becoming more lavish than the one before.

The end of the era arrived nearly twenty years later, due in large part to the introduction of the income tax. The Patersons vaunted, aristocratic lifestyle was never to be repeated. Over the next sixty years, Blantyre went through several transitions and changes in ownership, including an especially harsh and destructive period in the 1970s.

Things changed for the better when Jack and Jane Fitzpatrick bought the property in 1980. The Fitzpatricks also owned the well-respected Red Lion Inn in Stockbridge. They were determined to achieve the same standards for Blantyre and restore it to its original elegance.

After extensive renovations and the addition of many period pieces and fine furnishings, Blantyre was reopened in 1981. This small but impressive property reflected the vision of its new owners: a beautiful country house estate maintained as one of the finest hotels in the world so that guests could experience the service and splendor of a bygone era.

In 2000, ownership of Blantyre passed to their daughter, Ann Fitzpatrick Brown, who is following in her parents' footsteps, bringing her love of interior design and passion for perfection to bear on the estate. Today, the spa in the nineteenth-century building called the Potting Shed reflects the history and elegance of Blantyre.

"Wine brings to light the hidden secrets of the soul."

—Horace

Blantyre
P.O. Box 995
Lenox, MA 01240
(413) 637-3556

1/2 cup dates, chopped

3/4 cup water

1 teaspoon baking soda

1/2 cup butter

3/4 cup granulated sugar

2 eggs

Pinch of salt

3/4 cup all-purpose flour

1 tablespoon baking powder

STICKY TOFFEE SAUCE

3/4 cup dark brown sugar

2 tablespoons butter

1 cup heavy cream

1 1/2 teaspoons salt

Blantyre Sticky Toffee Pudding

Preheat oven to 350 degrees.

Bring dates, water, and baking soda to boil and let simmer about 2 minutes. Remove from heat and allow to cool to room temperature.

In mixer with paddle attachment, cream butter and sugar until pale. Slowly cream the eggs and salt. Fold in flour and baking powder; then fold in date/water mixture.

Spray ramekins with Pam and fill 3/4 full. Set in a deep pan and fill pan with water 2/3 of the way up. Cover pan with foil and, with a knife, make a few random holes. Bake for 30–40 minutes until puddings have risen a bit and become golden dark brown. Cool.

Turn puddings out of ramekins upside down onto a plate.

STICKY TOFFEE SAUCE

In a pot, simmer all ingredients on medium-low heat for about 2 hours until sauce is thickened. Ladle sauce over puddings. Top with whipped cream, ice cream, or the like.

PLATING

Rewarm the pudding and cover with sauce.

YIELD

Serves 7

Blantyre Candied Grapefruit Wedges

Peel 6 grapefruits, taking the pith with the peel. (Enjoy the segments for breakfast!)

Blanch peels in boiling water for 3–4 minutes.

Refresh immediately in cold water to cool. Perform these steps a total of 5 times, changing both the boiling water and the cold water each time.

Bring to a boil 1 cup water plus 1 cup sugar, then add in the grapefruit peels. (The peels must be submerged in the sugar/water syrup. If your grapefruit are very large, you may need to make more syrup.)

Cook slowly for about 2 hours until the whole is a sticky mass.

Cool just enough to handle and cut into shapes.

Refrigerate until time to serve.

Roll in granulated sugar just before serving.

Note: These keep in the refrigerator for a long time.

～ YIELD ～
Serves 8

6 grapefruits

1 cup water

1 cup sugar

1/2 cup sugar for rolling

8

2 medium-size green zucchini, bias-cut into 1/2-inch slices

1 teaspoon thyme

Salt and pepper to taste

Olive oil

Kernels from 2 ears of fresh corn on the cob

2 red peppers, cut into 1/2-inch-wide strips

Blantyre Zucchini with Corn and Peppers

Marinate zucchini, thyme, salt, and pepper in olive oil for 30 minutes.

Sauté the corn kernels in a skillet with a drizzle of olive oil for 1–2 minutes, seasoning to taste with salt and pepper. Cool.

Roast the peppers for a total of 12 minutes in a 375-degree oven.

Roast the zucchini only 6 minutes.

Bring all vegetables to room temperature to serve.

⤙ YIELD ⤚

Serves 4

Blantyre Roasted Chicken Breast with Vanilla Poached Citrus Salad

Segment all citrus (removing all peels and skins), discard seeds, and reserve the flesh. Gently hand-squeeze the peels and skins, retaining the juice.

Bring juice and vanilla to a boil, then allow to cool to room temperature.

Pour over fruit segments.

Allow to chill 24 hours.

PLATING

Lift the fruit from the juice, draining slightly and plate the fruit. Slice the chicken and place over the fruit. Drizzle juice over all.

Tip: Any extra juice is good in a vodka cocktail!

YIELD

Serves 4

4 cooked chicken breasts (roasted with salt and pepper) and cooled

1 pink grapefruit

2 blood oranges

2 navel oranges

2 lemons

1 lime

1 vanilla pod or 1 teaspoon vanilla extract

THE BOSTON PARK PLAZA HOTEL & TOWERS

Boston

In 1922, the great hotelier E. M. Statler purchased the triangular plot of land on which the hotel still sits for $450,000. This spot was once the beach from which British troops embarked on the trip that ended at the Battle of Lexington. Statler's goal was to create a grand American hotel that would make Bostonians proud to welcome visitors to the growing city. When the Boston Statler was built in 1927, it offered thirteen hundred guest rooms. It remained the largest independent hotel in all of New England for five decades and the eighth largest hotel in the world.

Called a "city within a city," the Boston Statler was built with approximately five million bricks of all kinds and contains forty miles of plumbing. The hotel's basement housed the largest barber shop in New England. The sidewalk around the hotel stretches more than a quarter of a mile. The entire third floor was devoted to the living and dining quarters of the hotel staff.

The house physician maintained an office and hospital on the hotel's fourteenth floor. The doctor observed regular office hours, but emergency cases were handled at any time. On the roof was a penthouse with two floors for service functions, including a print shop for the production of menus and incidental house literature, a carpenter shop, and an upholsterers shop.

The Boston Statler was the first hotel in the nation to outfit every guest room with radios. These radios would tune into only two programs, brought to the hotel from the rooftop broadcasting station of the Westinghouse Electrical and Manufacturing Company. Other Statler innovations included complimentary morning newspapers provided to guests under doors cut one inch short to allow quiet delivery, private bathrooms, light switches instead of pull chains, built-in closets, telephones in every room, reading lamps over the beds, writing desks with free pens and stationery, sewing kits and pin cushions as standard amenities, overnight "in-house" laundry service, mail chutes on each floor, electric razor outlets and a holder for used razor blades, and filtered, circulating ice water in every bathroom.

Statler's philosophy of service was formed when he was just fifteen and the head bellboy at the McLure House: "The guest is always right." He defined service as "the maximum of courteous and

efficient attention given by each employee to each individual guest." Statler's chant was "Courtesy. Cleanliness. Comfort." He once explained why he focused most on pleasing the guest: "Pleasing individual guests is at once the whole aim and the whole satisfaction to be derived from the industry."

The hotel was designed from the start for celebrations. The Imperial Ballroom, with its sparkling crystal chandeliers, gilded balconies, and proscenium arch stage, accommodates up to two thousand. A more intimate setting for fifty can be found in the historic Boston atmosphere of the oak-paneled Hancock Room. Enter the hotel's palatial Grand Lobby and you'll experience the grace and warmth that is its signature whether serving afternoon tea in Swan's Café or hosting a convention or gala dinner.

The grandeur and elegance of the hotel that Statler built has attracted a long list of heads of state, Hollywood stars, artists, authors, and sports figures. Some of the city's top restaurants can be found at the Boston Park Plaza Hotel & Towers, including Todd English's Bonfire Steakhouse, Swan's Café, Whiskey Park, McCormick & Schmick's Seafood Restaurant, and M. J. O'Connor's Irish Pub. There is a restaurant to suit virtually every taste.

Statler once remarked, "The three most important elements in any hotel's success are location, location, location." With an unmatched location for business and leisure travel, the Boston Park Plaza Hotel & Towers is adjacent to the Public Garden with its Swan Boats and Boston Common. Rich in history, the hotel offers guests the same hospitality and service that has attracted numerous presidents, international business leaders, and celebrities for almost a century.

"Part of the secret of success in life is to eat what you like, and let the food fight it out inside."

—Mark Twain

The Boston Park Plaza Hotel & Towers
Fifty Park Plaza at Arlington Street
Boston, MA 02116-3912
(617) 426-2000

1 side fresh salmon

1 teaspoon garlic, chopped

1/2 lemon

Freshly ground pepper

Dill sprig, coarsely chopped

1/2 cup Yin Hao jasmine tea

2/3 cup kosher salt

2/3 cup brown sugar

Tea-Cured Gravlax

Clean and rinse the fresh salmon with skin left on. Spread chopped garlic and squeeze lemon on salmon, then sprinkle with pepper and dill. Heavily layer tea on fish. Follow with a thick layer of mixed kosher salt and brown sugar. Place plastic wrap over fish and flip.

Repeat on the other side. If doing two sides, sandwich them together, then wrap in sandwich wrap. If doing one side only, wrap alone. Place salmon in hotel pan with another hotel pan on top. Place weights on the top pan; cans work well for weights. Refrigerate.

Flip fish in 12 hours. Check after 24 hours. You are looking for translucence and firmness to the touch. Timing will depend on the thickness of the fillet. When done, rinse well in cold water, being sure to support the fish the entire time so the flesh does not crack. Slice as needed.

YIELD

Serves 4

Spiced Apple Mar-Tea-Ni

INFUSED VODKA

Place 1 liter of vodka in nonreactive container. Add ginger slices, clove, and roughly chopped dried pear. Let steep at room temperature for 20 minutes then add the whole leaf black tea, preferably a good Ceylon or Chinese Congou. Taste periodically until proper strength is achieved (probably around 30 minutes after the tea was added). Strain multiple times through cheesecloth or coffee filters until completely clear. Store at room temperature.

DRINK RECIPE

In cocktail shaker filled with ice, shake 4 parts infused vodka with 1 part apple schnapps and a splash of Gran Marnier. Strain into a chilled martini glass. Garnish with a twist of lemon.

YIELD

1 mar-tea-ni

INFUSED VODKA

1 liter

12 quarter-sized slices of fresh ginger

1 whole clove

6 dried pear halves, roughly cut

1/3 cup of whole leaf black tea

DRINK RECIPE

4 parts infused vodka

1 part apple schnapps or other apple liquor

Splash of Cointreu or Gran Marnier

1 pound smoked bacon

2 ounces garlic, chopped

5 ounces capers

5 ounces anchovies, chopped

1 1/2 pounds onions, chopped

2 jalapeños, chopped

2 cinnamon sticks

1 quart raisins

1 quart red wine vinegar

1 1/2 cups molasses

1/2 pound dark brown sugar

1/2 cup Dijon mustard

1/2 cup tomato paste

3 cups tomatoes

1/2 cup Worcestershire sauce

Salt and pepper to taste

Bonfire Steak Sauce

Render bacon. Chop garlic, capers, and anchovies, and mix. Caramelize garlic, capers, and anchovies in bacon fat until toasty. Add onions, jalapeños, cinnamon sticks, and raisins. Deglaze with red wine vinegar and reduce.

Add molasses, sugar, mustard, tomato paste, and tomatoes. Reduce and add Worcestershire sauce. Cook out and adjust with salt and pepper. Remove cinnamon sticks. Purée and strain.

CANYON RANCH
Lenox

Twenty years ago we ventured off for a few nights to stay in Canyon Ranch in Lenox, Massachusetts, for our very first spa experience. It was a dazzling sight to see the famed architectural focal point of Canyon Ranch, which is the historic marble and brick Bellefontaine Mansion. The four-story mansion, built in 1897, is a copy of Louis XIV's Petit Trianon and was built by the architects who designed the New York City Public Library.

The mansion exterior has been restored to its original grandeur, while the interior has been fully renovated and contains the original library wing with its wood-and-marble-trimmed fireplace, ten-foot-high bookcases, a gracious dining room, and Café Tasse. The hallmark of Canyon Ranch is its fully staffed Health & Healing Center, located on the second and third floors of Bellefontaine Mansion.

The mansion also boasts a two-story solarium with conference facilities and two spacious guest lounges with fireplaces. The main buildings are the inn, the spa, and Bellefontaine Mansion, connected by all-weather, glass-enclosed walkways and arranged around the reflecting pool and formal gardens. Guests enjoy the magnificent views of rolling lawns and stately trees.

Canyon Ranch can accommodate 200 guests in the modern, two-story inn, which has two wings with 126 newly remodeled guest rooms and suites. Registration, guest services, a meditation room, meeting rooms, a computer center, and the Demonstration Kitchen are also located there.

Canyon Ranch, which opened in 1989, is world renowned for its life-enhancing vacations. Situated on 120 woodland acres, Canyon Ranch is 150 miles from New York City and 130 miles from Boston. Complimentary van transportation for guests is provided to and from Albany International airport, the Albany train station (Rensselaer, New York), and Bradley International Airport (Hartford, Connecticut).

In addition to more than fifty fitness classes and activities daily, Canyon Ranch offers an extensive outdoor sports program that includes group hiking, biking, tennis, canoeing, kayaking, sculling, snowshoeing, and downhill and cross-country skiing. Guests also find a variety of spiritual fitness classes.

Canyon Ranch offers in-depth preventive health-care assessments and guidance. Guests may choose private consultations or workshops in lifestyle change, transition, and stress management.

 *16*

Professional staff can prescribe personalized programs for disease prevention, weight loss, or smoking cessation. Guests interested in food planning may select healthy-cooking classes and nutrition consultations. Since 1979, Canyon Ranch has been celebrated as a leader in healthy gourmet cuisine. The Canyon Ranch kitchens are legendary for continual innovation, the quality and freshness of all ingredients, and great tastes. Guests can learn to cook healthy meals at home by attending daily Lunch & Learn demonstrations or Hands-On Cooking classes.

The heart of ranch activities is the one-hundred-thousand-square-foot spa complex with exercise, weight training, and cycling gyms; studios for yoga and Pilates/Gyrotonic; indoor tennis, racquetball, cycling, and squash courts; indoor and outdoor swimming pools; an indoor jogging track; massage and body treatment rooms; and skin-care and beauty salons.

Men's and women's locker rooms feature saunas, steam and inhalation rooms, whirlpools, a comfortable relaxation lounge, and fully equipped vanities. Outdoor facilities include a fifty-foot swimming pool, tennis courts, and a ropes challenge course. Miles of walking, hiking, biking, and cross-country ski trails are available both on Canyon Ranch grounds and in surrounding areas.

Canyon Ranch maintains a staff-to-guest ratio of nearly three to one. This includes physicians, nurses, behavioral therapists, exercise physiologists, nutritionists, movement therapists, acupuncturists, fitness instructors, tennis and racquetball pros, aestheticians, massage and bodywork therapists, art and music therapists, hiking and biking guides, and support staff.

Canyon Ranch guests may select from a variety of comprehensive vacation packages that include accommodations, three nutritionally balanced gourmet meals per day, use of spa and resort facilities, fitness classes and sports activities, educational wellness presentations, airport and train transfers, resorts amenities fees, and a selection of spa and health services based on length of stay. Award-winning Canyon Ranch, set among the wooded hills of Lenox, Massachusetts, offers the ultimate healthy vacation. At the turn of the twentieth century, the Berkshires was a haven for aristocrats. Owner and founder Mel Zuckerman has long been inspired by Jesse F. Williams, MD, whose words are at the core of the Canyon Ranch philosophy:

It's of value to think of health as that condition of the individual that makes possible the highest enjoyment of life. Health, when thought of simply as the absence of disease, is a standard of me-

diocrity, but when thought of as a quality of life is a standard of inspiration and ever-increasing achievement.

For me, our heartfelt intention to help every guest find greater joy in living is what makes us different from all other resorts. We want to connect this intention—our steadfast desire to inspire and motivate people to live well—with your goal of feeling great and living long. This is the reason Canyon Ranch exists, and we're very emotional about it. We have reason to believe that few of our guests "escape" entirely untouched. Your own *a-ha!* moment could happen during a consultation with a doctor or in a meditation class or somewhere out on a hiking trail—or you may connect your actions to your future well-being gradually, over the course of many visits.

Obviously, no one can "make" anyone live a more healthful life, and nothing could be less like boot camp than a Canyon Ranch stay. But you should know that with every meal, walk, massage, workshop, professional consult and fitness class, we are doing our level best to seduce you with the beauty of vibrant health.

Call Canyon Ranch to make a reservation for a minimum of a three-night stay, and enjoy the fine healthy food and life-changing environment of a sojourn at this historic property.

"I look upon it that he who does not mind his belly, will hardly mind anything else."

—Samuel Johnson

Canyon Ranch in Lenox, Mass.
165 Kemble Street
Lenox, MA 01240
(800) 742-9000

Canola oil

1 small zucchini, sliced 1/2-inch
thick in half-moon shapes

1 small yellow squash, sliced
1/2-inch thick in half-moon
shapes

1 Roma tomato, diced

1 small onion, diced

1/2 cup frozen corn

1 teaspoon fresh oregano,
chopped

1/2 teaspoon freshly ground black
pepper

1/2 teaspoon sea salt

Calabacitas

Preheat oven to 425 degrees. Lightly coat a sheet pan with canola oil.

Lay zucchini and yellow squash on sheet pan and roast in oven for 5–10 minutes, or until golden brown.

Lightly coat a sauté pan with canola oil. Add roasted squash, tomatoes, onions, and corn. Sauté over medium heat until just soft, about 5 minutes. Add oregano, salt, and pepper to taste. Serve immediately.

YIELD

4 half-cup servings

Red Lentil Soup

Heat olive oil in a large saucepan over medium heat. Sauté onions, carrots, celery, and garlic until onions are translucent.

Add vegetable stock, lentils, and herbs. Bring to a boil, reduce heat, and simmer for 1 hour, or until lentils are soft.

Remove from heat, cool slightly, and pour into a blender container. Purée until smooth. Add vinegar, Worcestershire, salt, and pepper and mix well.

YIELD

6 three-quarter-cup servings

1 tablespoon olive oil

1/2 cup onions, chopped

1/4 cup carrots, chopped

1/4 cup celery, chopped

1 tablespoon garlic, minced

1 1/2 quarts vegetable stock

1 cup red lentils

1/4 teaspoon dried basil

Pinch of dried oregano

Pinch of dried thyme

1 1/2 teaspoons white distilled vinegar

1/2 teaspoon Worcestershire sauce

1 teaspoon salt

1/4 teaspoon ground black pepper

 *20*

Canola oil

1/3 cup butter

2/3 cup low-fat cream cheese

1 1/2 cups brown sugar

1 egg yolk

1/3 cup black strap molasses

1 1/2 cups all-purpose flour

3/4 cup whole wheat flour

1/2 teaspoon ground ginger

1 1/2 teaspoons baking soda

1/4 teaspoon salt

2 tablespoons fresh ginger root, peeled and minced

1/2 cup crystallized ginger, minced

Triple Ginger Cookies

Preheat oven to 350 degrees. Lightly coat a baking sheet with canola oil.

In a large mixing bowl, cream the butter, cream cheese, and brown sugar on low speed with an electric mixer. Add egg yolk and molasses, and mix on low until just combined.

In a large bowl, combine dry ingredients. Add to butter mixture and mix on low for 10–20 seconds. Add fresh ginger and crystallized ginger. Mix briefly by hand. Portion heaping teaspoonfuls (or use a 3/4-ounce scoop) onto baking sheet about 1 1/2 inches apart. Bake for 7 minutes. Rotate baking sheet and bake an additional 2 minutes.

YIELD

3 dozen

CHATHAM BARS INN
Chatham

Chatham Bars Inn has been New England's premier oceanfront resort and a renowned Cape Cod landmark since its opening in 1914. This turn-of-the-century main inn sits gracefully atop a rise overlooking Pleasant Bay and the open Atlantic, while luxurious Cape-style cottages, offering from one to eighteen bedrooms, dot the surrounding landscape.

The property on which Chatham Bars Inn and the golf course are located was originally part of the Sears family homestead in the 1700s. The last Sears member to own and operate the farmland was the Honorable Richard Sears, known in his day as "Squire Sears." Richard was born in Chatham in 1749. When he was eleven, his father passed away, and he moved with his mother to Boston after she remarried. At the age of thirteen, Richard moved back to Chatham and lived under the care of Gen. Joseph Otis. When Richard came of adult age, he became the largest real estate owner in Chatham. Along with running the farm, Richard also owned a variety store and was engaged in saltworks.

Richard Sears held many prominent positions throughout his life. He was coroner in 1781 and justice of the court and justice of the peace in 1814. He was the elected town representative to the general court eleven times between 1780 and 1814. He also served as senator, town clerk, treasurer, and lieutenant of the town militia during the Revolutionary War. Mr. Sears died in 1839 at the age of ninety.

In 1912, Charles Ashley Hardy began to purchase the land where the hotel and golf course are now located with the hope of opening a hunting lodge for Boston vacationers. When Chatham Bars Inn opened on June 14, 1914, it catered to the hunting crowd and considered itself a hunting lodge. Bird shooting was probably the most popular sport, but fox was also widely hunted. Nat A. Eldredge, the first general manager of Chatham Bars Inn, led guests on fox hunts in the Chatham and Monomoy area. They also hunted quail, waterfowl, and plover.

The increase of hunting and the amount of commercial hunting of waterfowl and shorebirds for markets and millinery trade threatened to render some bird populations extinct. The Federal Migratory Bird Treaty was passed in 1916, putting an end to the hunting of fowl. The fox hunts continued into the 1930s.

The main inn and nine of the surrounding eighteen cottages were designed and built by Boston architect Harvey Bailey Alden. William H. Cox was the architect of the other nine original cottages.

The style was typical of the local resort architecture of the day. Early advertisements boasted of "plastered, soundproof rooms with electric lights. Steam Heat, and long distance telephone in every room. Private bath-rooms, with fresh and salt (ocean) water baths. Sun deck, with every second story front room. Fire-proof fire escapes."

The cuisine was considered "the best of New England cooking with special attention to seafood." They offered "clean dairy milk, cream and butter, and fruit and vegetables from model Cape Cod farms." For many years the vegetables were grown in the hotel gardens, where Greensleeves Nursery now resides. An early dinner menu reveals a variety of local shellfish and game delicacies, as well as two rather curious New England dishes, Yorkshire Buck and Yarmouth Bloaters.

The inn also offered "a modern, fire-proof garage for eighty cars." This garage was located on Chatham Bars Avenue, where the storage center is now located. The resort guests could enjoy the sandy beach, clay tennis courts, fishing, sailing, motor boating, and yacht racing. They also had "unexcelled surf and pool bathing, with varying temperatures, in ocean water free from seaweed." The hotel had a pier that stretched from the hotel beach over a natural pool of salt water to an emerged sandbar.

Famous individuals who have stayed at the inn include Henry Ford, Henry Morganthau, William Rockefeller, and the Dutch royal family, who spent part of their World War II exile at Chatham Bars Inn.

When Charles Hardy died on November 30, 1929, from a fatal hunting accident in Chatham, the management of the hotel was continued by the Chatham Associates, a trust company incorporated in January 1916 by Charles Hardy and his associates. The resort continued to maintain the gracious style and attentive service that earned it the status of one of America's premier oceanfront resorts.

In 1953 the associates of the Chatham Trust sold the hotel and property to E. R. McMullen, a long-time summer resident. After thirty-three years of service, McMullen sold Chatham Bars Inn to William Langelier in 1986–1987. Langelier and his partner Alan Green were the first owners to keep the hotel open year-round. The partners invested over $2 million in capital improvements.

In 1994 the resort was purchased by Great American Life Insurance Company. At that time a multiyear, multi-million-dollar restoration project commenced and continues today.

Chatham Bars Inn is one of a handful of resorts, hotels, and inns recognized as a destination of significant value by the National Preservation of Historic Trusts and Historic Hotels of America.

The resort's 205 rooms and suites combine the best of past and present in everything from fireplaces and exquisite hand-painted furniture to nightly turndown service and wireless Internet access. Amenities include the luxury of a quarter mile of private sandy beach, an outdoor pool, a complimentary children's program, four award-winning restaurants, beachside clambakes and barbecues, seven impressive meeting rooms, tennis courts, a spa, and adjacent golf, all on twenty-five splendid acres. It is a short stroll to the charming village of Chatham with its many historic sites, unique shops, and galleries.

"The only real stumbling block is fear of failure. In cooking you've got to have a what-the-hell attitude."

—Julia Child

Chatham Bars Inn
297 Shore Road
Chatham, MA 02633
(508) 945-6778
www.chathambarsinn.com

Chatham Bars Inn Clam Chowder

1/4 pound unsalted butter

1 cup Spanish onion, chopped

1 cup celery, chopped

1/3 cup flour

3 cans chopped clams,
    6 1/2 ounces each

4 bottles clam juice, 8 ounces each

2 ounces salt pork, scored

1 teaspoon clam base or
    2 medium clam
    bouillon cubes

2 cups potato, diced and cooked

1 pint half-and-half, warmed

Salt and pepper to taste

In a large saucepan or soup pot, melt the butter; sauté onion and celery until translucent. Stir in flour, cook for 5 minutes.

Drain clams, reserving juice; add juice to the bottled clam juice. Set clams aside. Add clam juice to the saucepan and whisk until smooth. Add salt pork, clam base, and chopped clams; cook for 20 minutes.

Add cooked potatoes. Let stand for 20 minutes. Remove and discard salt pork. Stir in cream. Season with salt and pepper.

YIELD

12 servings

Chocolate Peanut Butter Crunch Cake with Peanut Brittle and Chocolate Sauce

CHOCOLATE CAKE

Whisk together cocoa powder and boiling water. Set aside. Cream together butter and brown sugar until fluffy. Add egg and vanilla extract. Scrape well. Add flour, baking soda, and salt. Scrape again. Add cocoa powder/water mixture. Scrape again. Add sour cream. Pour into parchment-paper-lined 9-inch round pan. Bake at 350 degrees for 20 minutes. Cool and chill. Trim top of cake. Place in 9" × 2.5" cake ring.

CRUNCH FILLING

Melt chocolate and peanut butter over double boiler. Fold in feuilletine. Spread on top of chocolate cake. Freeze.

CHOCOLATE MOUSSE

Melt chocolate and butter over double boiler. Set aside. Whip heavy cream until soft. Chill.

Whisk together eggs and sugar in mixing bowl over double boiler until warm to the touch and sugar has dissolved. Place on mixer and whip until thick and light in color (approximately 5 minutes). By hand, whisk in chocolate/butter mixture. Fold in whipped cream. Spread on top of crunch layer. Freeze 20 minutes.

CHOCOLATE CAKE

1/2 ounce dark cocoa powder

3 ounces boiling water

2 ounces butter

5 ounces brown sugar

1 egg

1 teaspoon vanilla extract

2 1/2 ounces flour

1 teaspoon baking soda

1/4 teaspoon salt

2 1/2 ounces sour cream

CRUNCH FILLING

4 ounces bittersweet chocolate, chopped

4 1/2 ounces creamy peanut butter

4 ounces feuilletine (crushed wafer cookies) or 13 ounces Rice Krispies

CHOCOLATE MOUSSE

7 ounces bittersweet chocolate, chopped

1 ounce butter

8 ounces heavy cream

2 eggs

4 1/2 ounces sugar

PEANUT BUTTER MOUSSE

8 ounces heavy cream

8 ounces cream cheese

4 1/2 ounces confectioners' sugar

4 1/2 ounces creamy peanut
    butter

GANACHE

6 ounces heavy cream

6 ounces bittersweet chocolate,
    chopped

2/3 cup toasted, salted peanuts

PEANUT BRITTLE

8 ounces butter

1 tablespoon light corn syrup

1 tablespoon water

8 ounces sugar

5 ounces toasted, salted peanuts

CHOCOLATE SAUCE

1/2 ounce water

1 1/2 ounces butter

2 ounces sugar

1 1/2 ounces light corn syrup

1/2 ounces bittersweet chocolate,
    chopped

1/3 ounce dark cocoa powder

SIDING

2/3 cup toasted, salted peanuts,
    chopped

PEANUT BUTTER MOUSSE

Whip cream until soft. Set aside. Beat together cream cheese and confectioners' sugar until soft. Add peanut butter. Scrape well. Add whipped cream. Spread on top of chocolate mousse layer. Freeze 2 1/2 to 3 hours.

GANACHE

Heat cream. Add to chocolate. Whisk together.

Unmold cake and place on cardboard circle on plate. Place on rack. Pour ganache over top and spread onto sides. Coat side of cake with 2/3 cup toasted, salted peanuts. Chill.

PEANUT BRITTLE

Melt butter over low heat. Add corn syrup, water, and sugar. Cook, stirring occasionally, to hard crack stage (290 degrees) and until amber in color. Remove from heat. Stir in peanuts. Pour onto parchment-paper-lined baking sheet. Cool and break into pieces.

CHOCOLATE SAUCE

Bring water, butter, sugar, and corn syrup to a boil. Whisk in chocolate and cocoa powder. Boil 1 minute. Remove from heat. Let cool to room temperature, approximately 1 1/2 hours.

PLATING

Using a hot knife, cut cake into 12 slices. On plate, drizzle cake with chocolate sauce. Place a piece of peanut brittle on top.

~€ YIELD ℈~

12 servings

CONCORD'S COLONIAL INN

Concord

—❧————————————————————————————❧—

Concord has a unique place in American history. The "shot heard round the world" was fired on April 19, 1775, at the Old North Bridge in Concord. The opening stanza of Ralph Waldo Emerson's "Concord Hymn" describes the impact of the ensuing battle.

Then, in the mid-nineteenth century, Concord was the center of the country's literary renaissance and home to some of the nation's most influential writers, such as Ralph Waldo Emerson, Henry David Thoreau, Louisa May Alcott, and Nathaniel Hawthorne.

First settled by the English colonists in 1635, Concord was primarily an agricultural community until the twentieth century. Although farmlands have diminished in recent decades, the area has maintained its rural features. Extensive parklands, meandering rivers, and gently rolling hills preserve the natural beauty that inspired Thoreau's *Walden* and Emerson's "Nature."

Records show that the original owner of the land where the Colonial Inn sits was Peter Bulkeley, one of the original settlers. Bulkeley's widow sold the property to Captain Timothy Wheeler, who left it to his daughter, Rebecca, in 1687. Rebecca was married to Captain James Minot, who built the East House in the late 1600s. Captain Minot left the house to his son, James Jr., who lived there for a while, then left it to his son, Ephraim, in 1759 when he died.

In 1764, Ephraim sold the property to his cousin, Dr. Timothy Minot. During the battle of the Old North Bridge, Dr. Minot tended the wounded. During the Minot ownership, the Central Building was erected at the west end of East House. It was used as a provincial storehouse during the Revolution.

Deacon John White purchased the new building for a store in 1780 and lived in one end of it. The variety store specialized in paints and oils but also carried general merchandise. In 1789, Dr. Minot sold the East House to his son-in-law, Ammi White, the cabinet maker who, as a boy, killed the third British solder at the bridge with an axe. Ammi added a long shop, or shed, to his East House. On this same day, Dr. Minot sold the Central Building to Deacon White.

In 1799, Ammi White sold his East House to John Thoreau (1754–1801) of Boston. When Thoreau died, his widow continued to live in the house. His boy, John, became the father of Henry David Thoreau. Around 1821, Daniel Shattuck bought the Central Building and the store. He also

helped found the Middlesex Insurance Company, the National Bank, the Savings Bank, and the Milldam Company.

From 1835 to 1837, Henry David Thoreau, his parents, and family lived in West House while Henry was a student at Harvard. When Betsy Thoreau died in 1839, Dan Shattuck bought the East House and then converted the store into a dwelling in 1850. In 1855, the Central Building became a boarding house. Soon, this building was attached to East House, and the combination was run as a small hotel called Thoreau House. Around 1900, West House was attached to the Central Building and was managed by Mr. and Mrs. Abrams, who gave the entire structure its present name, Colonial Inn.

In 1947, ownership of the inn was taken over by Luther and Loring Grimes. Loring added the Prescott Wing in 1960 and the dining room in 1973. In 1988, when hotelier Jurgen Demisch became proprietor, he became caretaker of a landmark that is often a visitor's first introduction to Concord. With his wife, Rebecca, he undertook major renovations and redecorated the inn, and patrons welcomed the high standards for food and service.

Concord's Colonial Inn
48 Monument Square
Concord, MA 01742
(978) 369-9200
(800) 370-9200

2 quarts half-and-half

1 stick unsalted butter

4 ounces white sugar

8 ounces cornmeal, yellow,
    fine to medium

8 ounces molasses

1/4 teaspoon ground cinnamon

1/4 teaspoon ground nutmeg

1/4 teaspoon ground ginger

1 teaspoon salt

8 whole eggs, beaten

Whipped cream or vanilla
    ice cream

Colonial Inn's Famous Indian Pudding

Preheat oven to 300 degrees.

Bring half-and-half, butter, and sugar to a light boil.

Add cornmeal and cook for a few minutes. Lower fire to low to medium.

Add molasses, cinnamon, nutmeg, ginger, salt, and eggs.

Pour pudding into an oven-safe dish and cover it with foil. Bake the pudding for about 45 minutes, or until its center reaches 165 degrees.

Serve with whipped cream or vanilla ice cream.

YIELD

20 servings

Pumpkin Crème Brûlée

Preheat oven to 325 degrees.

You will need 6 oven-safe six- to eight-ounce ramekins set in a water bath. (Put the ramekins in an oven-safe dish that is able to fit the ramekins with water going halfway up the sides of the dish.)

Put cream, sugar, pumpkin purée, vanilla beans, and salt into a two-quart saucepan. Place this mixture on a medium flame until it begins to simmer.

Whisk the egg yolks together gently in a bowl. Do not put any air into them.

Add a few ounces of the hot cream mixture to the eggs and gently stir. Add a little more cream until you have added half.

Add the eggs and cream to the rest of the hot cream and stir gently.

Fill your ramekins so there is about 1 inch of space left on the top.

Bake your brûlées at 325 degrees for roughly 45 minutes, or until the center is firm and not liquid.

Cool your brûlées overnight if possible in the refrigerator. Discard the water and baking pan.

1 quart heavy or whipping cream

1 cup white sugar

1/2 can pumpkin purée

1 vanilla bean, split

Pinch of salt

8 egg yolks

1 whole egg

Sprinkle the brûlées with white sugar and burn the top with a kitchen blowtorch.

Serve with fresh berries and/or a nice crisp cookie.

YIELD

6 servings

Colonial Inn Fork Tender Pot Roast

Preheat oven to 250 degrees.

Sear the eye of the round in a hot heavy-bottomed pan until it is brown and caramelized.

Take it out and caramelize the onions, celery, and carrots.

Add the tomato paste and cook with the vegetables for 3 minutes.

Return the meat to the pan. Add the beef broth and canned tomatoes and cover with water until the liquid reaches 3/4 of the way up the sides of the meat. Add the bay leaves.

Braise at 250 degrees for 8–10 hours, turning the meat over every hour. Braise it until it is fork tender.

Serve the pot roast with the braising sauce. Add some salt and pepper to taste.

The key to great pot roast is to sear the meat well, getting it nice and brown on the outside. Next, you want to get good color on your vegetables. The most important step is to be patient. If you wait the 10 hours, you will be cutting your pot roast with a fork, so remember,

---

1 eye of the round choice beef

2 onions, diced

1/2 head celery, diced

2 carrots, diced

1/2 can tomato paste

1 can (14 ounces) tomato, chopped

2 cans beef stock or broth

2 bay leaves

good things come to those who wait. One more suggestion: wait until the end for your salt and pepper. As the liquid reduces, it may become too salty if you add the salt too early.

❦ YIELD ❧

6–8 servings

CRANWELL RESORT, SPA AND GOLF CLUB

Lenox

Strolling around the grounds of Cranwell Resort is a walk through history. In 1853, Rev. Henry Ward Beecher purchased what was then called Blossom Hill, where the Cranwell mansion now stands, for $4,500. He loved the views, and from this vantage point, he proclaimed, "From here I can see the very hills of Heaven." These same views can be seen today when you sit on the Rose Terrace at dusk and are reminded of the legendary parties that took place on this same property some hundred years ago.

If Reverend Beecher's name sounds vaguely familiar it is because Harriet Beecher Stowe, the author of the antislavery novel *Uncle Tom's Cabin*, was his sister. But the reverend was famous in his own right. He was active in the women's suffrage and antislavery movements.

In 1847, Reverend Beecher was appointed the first minister of the new Plymouth Congregational Church in Brooklyn, New York. He had presidential aspirations, which might have been fulfilled from one of the most prominent pulpits in America, but his dreams were ended by a scandalous affair. In the highly publicized scandal known as the Beecher-Tilton Affair, the reverend was publicly tried on charges that he had committed adultery with a friend's wife, Elizabeth Tilton. Despite several bouts of legal activity, Beecher was never convicted, although both Elizabeth Tilton and her husband were eventually excommunicated from the church.

Gen. John F. Rathbone purchased Blossom Hill from Beecher in 1869 and began construction by moving Beecher's farmhouse to the side so that the new home would have the commanding view of the countryside. The home Rathbone built, Wyndhurst, was enormous by any standards of the day. Ironically, these palatial homes were called "cottages."

In 1882, another family was building yet another "cottage" on the backside of the hill. U.S. Navy captain John S. Barnes, who had served as flag officer of the North Atlantic Fleet during the Civil War, purchased the land for $10,000 and erected Coldbrooke, now known as Beecher's Cottage and part of the Cranwell property.

The next owner of the property was John Sloane, a relative of the Vanderbilts and co-owner of the famous furniture firm W&J Sloane. He built his "cottage" in 1894. After tearing down Rathbone's Wyndhurst and Beecher's farmhouse, Sloane constructed another Wyndhurst, which rivaled

the first in enormity and elegance. He also commissioned Frederick Law Olmsted, the landscape architect who created New York's Central Park and the Boston area's Emerald Necklace, to design the grounds. It is this new version of Wyndhurst that stands on the hill today.

When Sloane's daughter sold the estate to a group of Florida developers in 1925, the property was briefly run as the Berkshire Hunt and Country Club. Edward Cranwell then purchased it in 1930 and later gave the estate to the Society of Jesus of New England in 1939. It was turned into a private school for boys named after the generous benefactor. After thriving for many years, the school eventually slipped into decline, closing its doors in 1975.

The Cranwell of today is set on 380 acres, and much of its original grandeur has been restored. The resort has 107 deluxe rooms situated in various buildings: the Carriage House, Founder's Cottage, Olmsted Manor, Beecher's Cottage (formerly Coldbrooke), and the Mansion (formerly the new version of Wyndhurst). Cranwell is also home to the Spa at Cranwell, one of the largest spas in the Northeast.

The *Golf Digest* golf school's staff of PGA pros offers professional instruction at its training facility. The eighteen-hole golf course is the original designed by Stiles & Van Cleek. In the winter, snow turns the course into a cross-country skier's delight.

Exquisite cuisine is served in Cranwell's award-winning Wyndhurst and the Music Room, while casual fare can be found in Sloane's Tavern year round. This hotel and resort is unique to the Northeast.

Over the years, Cranwell has served as a home to wealthy industrialists, clergy, writers, students, golfers, and culture lovers. The centerpiece of the property, with its extraordinary views of the Berkshires, is still the hilltop Tudor-style mansion, which has dominated the countryside for more than a century. The history of Cranwell is entwined with many stories of the opulent period between 1880 and 1920 known as the Gilded Age. Cranwell Resort is a member of the prestigious National Trust Historic Hotels of America.

Cranwell Resort, Spa and Golf Club
55 Lee Road
Lenox, MA 01240
(413) 637-1364
(800) 272-6935

Baby Spinach Salad with Buttermilk Herb Dressing

In a bowl, whisk together the buttermilk, lemon juice, and olive oil. Add the shallots, dill, parsley, salt, and pepper and whisk.

Place spinach in a large salad bowl. Toss with enough dressing to cover greens. Place salad on platter. Top with orange segments and blue cheese.

YIELD

Serves 4–6

1/2 cup buttermilk

Juice of 1 lemon

1 teaspoon olive oil

1 tablespoon shallots, minced

2 teaspoons fresh dill, chopped

Salt and pepper to taste

2 teaspoons fresh parsley, chopped

1 pound baby spinach

2 mandarin oranges, segmented

2 ounces blue cheese crumbles

4 four-ounce boneless, skinless salmon fillets

1 pound Yukon Gold potatoes

1 pound spinach

Fresh thyme sprigs

ARTICHOKE LEMON VINAIGRETTE

2 tablespoons olive oil

1 tablespoon Cajun seasoning

2 tablespoons Dijon mustard

Juice of 2 lemons

2 teaspoons lemon zest

2 tablespoons fresh thyme

3/4 cup vegetable stock or water

1 cup artichoke hearts, chopped

Chilled Filet of Salmon, Braised Spinach, Yukon Gold Potatoes, and Artichoke Lemon Vinaigrette

Roast salmon fillets at 375 degrees for 8–10 minutes. Refrigerate.

Slice and blanch potatoes until al dente.

Steam or braise spinach until wilted.

ARTICHOKE LEMON VINAIGRETTE

Place all vinaigrette ingredients except artichokes into a mixing bowl and whisk together. Add chopped artichokes.

PLATING

Arrange potatoes on plate as first layer. Place cooked spinach as a "bed" for the salmon in the middle of the potato layer, leaving uncovered potatoes surrounding the spinach. Place cooked salmon on top of spinach. Drizzle vinaigrette over arrangement. Garnish with fresh thyme sprigs.

YIELD

Serves 4

Curried Chicken Salad with Whole Wheat Pita

Cook chicken breast one day ahead of preparing salad and refrigerate. Cut chicken breast into medium-sized diced pieces.

In a mixing bowl, combine oil, curry powder, salt, cayenne, garlic, lime juice, nonfat mayo, and sour cream and mix well.

Add onion, apple, and raisins and mix well.

Serve on platter of baby greens with halved whole wheat pita.

YIELD

Serves 8

2 pounds boneless, skinless chicken breast

2 tablespoons canola oil

2 tablespoons curry powder

1 teaspoon salt

1 teaspoon cayenne pepper

2 tablespoons garlic, minced

Juice of 2 limes

2 cups nonfat mayo

1/2 cup sour cream

1 cup red onion, diced

2 cups Granny Smith apple, cored and diced

2 cups raisins

Whole wheat pita bread

THE CROWNE POINTE HISTORIC INN & SPA

Provincetown

When the Pilgrims arrived in North America in 1620, they sailed into Cape Cod Bay and landed first at the tip of Cape Cod's distinctive peninsula at a place now called Provincetown. Noting that previous attempts at colonization had run into difficulty due to lack of government, they created and signed the Mayflower Compact in the bay, then proceeded to establish their settlement across the bay at Plymouth.

Having previously served as a seasonal fishing site for Native Americans, Provincetown developed into a bustling seaport inhabited by a rowdy mix of smugglers, outlaws, and raucous mariners. In more modern times, the town has evolved into a resort area with a unique aura. Combine the energy of South Beach with the friendliness of San Francisco, throw in the earthiness of a Greek village, and you get a sense of the town's charm.

Many well-known figures such as Jackson Pollock, Mark Rothko, Eugene O'Neill, Tennessee Williams, and Sinclair Lewis have called Provincetown home. This free-spirited community is a vital mix of artists, fishermen, and tourists. The result is a diverse and vibrant population that proudly honors its heritage while welcoming visitors from all walks of life.

Provincetown offers a variety of options for relaxation. You can laze away the day at the beach, seek out the solitude of the spectacular dunes, or just relax at the pool or spa with a cold drink. Or you can stroll, people-watch, shop, and examine art in the many shops. Other options include riding a bike or a horse through the dunes and many trails, sailing, whale watching, or just enjoying a sunrise or sunset over the ocean.

Long known for its unique brand of liberalism and its eccentric population, Provincetown advertises itself as one of the most tolerant communities in America. It has become quite popular for those with alternative lifestyles that would no doubt send the original colonists back out to sea in search of another landing spot.

The stately mansion that is now the main house of the Crowne Pointe Historic Inn & Spa was built near the turn of the nineteenth century for a prosperous sea captain of the Provincetown Harbor. The carriage houses that stand behind the main residence, which are believed to have housed numerous fishermen once upon a time, were constructed shortly after.

Since the early 1920s, when it began to take in travelers, the main house has been known as a place where visitors can rest their heads. Over the decades, as Provincetown became less the bustling harbor town and more the vibrant resort village, the mansion and carriage houses underwent many alterations until the current owners purchased the properties in January 1999.

The new owners, both builders and restoration enthusiasts, saw a "diamond in the rough." They viewed the property as their chance to pursue a life-long dream. They launched an elaborate restoration and full-scale renovation of the five buildings that now constitute Crowne Pointe. With only four months until high season, all hands turned industriously to the main house for its antici-pated opening in May of that year.

While the clock was ticking, construction crews worked seven days a week, from sun up until long past sun down, in an effort to put Crowne Pointe back together. At times, as many as sixty people were working on the site. At the end of a shift, one painting crew would leave the scaffolding only to let the next crew on.

No stone was left unturned in the detail category, from paint colors and authentic Victorian wallpapers to garden flowers, to the carefully restored banister of the parlor staircase, the graceful coffered tin and wood moldings, and the antique belt-driven fans on the newly expanded two-story front porch.

The Crowne Pointe family welcomes you to enjoy the handsome fruition of their dream. Whether you choose to come in the summer for the sand and surf of the nearby beaches and harbor or you prefer the quieter shoulder seasons in which to enjoy the charm and history of Provincetown, your stay at Crowne Pointe will be an unforgettable experience.

"I hate people who are not serious about their meals."

—Oscar Wilde

The Crowne Pointe Historic Inn & Spa
82 Bradford Street
Provincetown, MA 02657
(508) 487-6767

4 large eggs

3/4 cup whole milk

3/4 cup heavy cream

7 tablespoons sugar

2 tablespoons dark rum

4 tablespoons unsalted butter,
    room temperature

8 slices white bread

1 pint fresh strawberries, hulled
    and cut in half

Crowne Pointe Bread Pudding

In a medium bowl, whisk together eggs, milk, cream, 3 tablespoons sugar, and rum. Set aside.

Spread a generous amount of butter on the top of each slice of bread. Cut slices in half diagonally. In a 9-inch round baking dish or cake pan, fan overlapping bread slices in one layer. (It is also fine for bread to overlap randomly.) Pour egg mixture over bread and let stand 1 hour.

Preheat oven to 400 degrees. Sprinkle pudding with 2 tablespoons sugar. Bake until puffed and golden brown and pudding has set, about 20 minutes.

Meanwhile, in a medium bowl, combine strawberries with remaining 2 tablespoons sugar. Let stand while pudding bakes. Serve strawberries with baked pudding.

YIELD

Serves 4–6

Crowne Pointe
Molasses Drop Cookies

Preheat oven to 375 degrees. Line baking sheets with parchment paper. Set aside.

In a medium bowl, whisk together flour, baking soda, cloves, ginger, cinnamon, and salt. Set aside.

In the bowl of an electric mixer fitted with the paddle attachment, combine shortening and 1 cup sugar. Beat on medium speed until light and fluffy, about 2 minutes. Add egg and molasses, and beat to combine. Add dry ingredients, and beat on low to combine.

Place the remaining 1/2 cup sugar in a small bowl. Using a one-and-a-half-inch ice-cream scoop, form balls of dough. Roll dough balls between the palms of your hands until smooth. Roll in sugar. Place about 2 inches apart on prepared baking sheets. Bake until the cookies are set in the center and begin to crack, about 12 minutes, rotating the baking sheets once after 5 minutes. Transfer the baking sheets to a wire rack to cool for 5 minutes. Transfer cookies to rack until completely cool. Store in an airtight container for up to 1 week.

YIELD

About 50 cookies

2 cups all-purpose flour

2 teaspoons baking soda

1 teaspoon ground cloves

1 teaspoon ground ginger

1 teaspoon ground cinnamon

1/4 teaspoon salt

3/4 cup solid vegetable shortening

1 1/2 cups granulated sugar

1 large egg

1/4 cup unsulfured molasses

2 ten-inch flour tortillas

6 large eggs, lightly beaten (you may substitute 5 egg whites and 1 egg yolk)

Coarse salt and freshly ground pepper

1 tablespoon unsalted butter

1/4 cup fresh cilantro leaves

1/4 cup shredded Monterey Jack cheese

Tomatillo avocado salsa

Breakfast burrito pico de gallo

Crowne Pointe
Yummy Breakfast Burrito

Heat tortillas directly over gas flame or in a large skillet, turning frequently until heated through and softened. Set aside.

Whisk eggs in a medium bowl. Season with salt and pepper. In a medium nonstick skillet, melt butter over medium-high heat. When the butter is melted and foamy, add the eggs. Reduce heat to medium. Sprinkle with the cilantro and cheese. Using a rubber spatula or a flat wooden spoon, push eggs toward the center while tilting the skillet to distribute runny parts. Cook to desired consistency. Remove from skillet.

Divide eggs between tortillas. Top with salsa and *pico de gallo* (reserving extra salsa and *pico de gallo* for another use). Fold the tortillas over the filling to enclose. Serve immediately.

YIELD

Serves 2

DURGIN-PARK
Boston

Durgin-Park dates back to pre-Revolutionary days, when in 1742 Peter Faneuil was called the "top-most merchant" in the entire town. He erected a very large market house near the waterfront. Later a warehouse, the building now comprising the restaurant was constructed. A small eating place became a popular site for market men and crews of all the ships anchored in the harbor to gather and eat Yankee down-home food.

About 130 years ago, Eldredge Park, the owner of a livery stable nearby, bought the restaurant and formed a partnership with John Durgin, a commission merchant, and John Chandler, a young dry goods merchant. Sadly, a few years later Durgin and Park, who gave their names to the restaurant, died. John Chandler kept the name for sentimental reasons. It became a gustatory epitaph to his late partners.

Chandler proved to know his lobster and cods and set a generous helping of apple pie. For sixty-three years he served great food and even expanded the kitchen and restaurant to accommodate his great following. He loved going from his home in Milton each morning to buy the freshest ingredients for the restaurant. His son and grandson joined him in the business, but when Jerry Chandler was killed in the war, John sold to James Hallett.

In 135 years, the restaurant has changed chefs only three times; its historic menu remains practically the same. It is proud to serve market men, tourists, celebrities, and locals alike. With its sharp-tongued waitresses, clattering dishes, and incredible quantities of food, this place has the history and ambience of old Boston. In winter, bear steak is on the menu with turkey, venison pie, raccoon, and baked beans. Patrons love the blueberry cake and strawberry shortcake.

Barrels, boxes, and crates are stacked on the sidewalk, and the walk upstairs to the dining rooms is through a narrow entrance, but it's worth the time to dine at one of America's finest and best eateries.

James eats his meals at the restaurant most nights, and his brother became the chief bean man, a century-old position carrying with it the weighty responsibility of preparing the hundred-year-old recipe for true Boston baked beans.

 *46*

"There is no such thing as a little garlic."

—Anonymous

Durgin Park

340 Faneuil Hall Market Place

Boston, MA 02109

(617) 227-2038

Just a Boy

Got to understand the lad—
He's not eager to be bad;
If the right he always knew,
He would be as old as you.
Were he now exceeding wise,
He'd be just about your size;
When he does things that annoy,
Don't forget he's just a boy.

Being just a boy he'll do
Much you will not want him to;
He'll be careless of his ways.
Have his disobedient days.
Willful, wild and headstrong, too,
He'll need guidance kind and true;
Things of value he'll destroy,
But reflect—he's just a boy.

Could he know and understand,
He would need no guiding hand;
But he's young and hasn't learned
How life's corners must be turned.
Doesn't know from day to day
There is more to life than play.
More to face than selfish joy.
Don't forget—he's just a boy.

Just a boy who needs a friend,
Patient, kindly to the end;
Needs a father who will show
Him the things he wants to know,
Take him with you when you walk,
Listen when he wants to talk,
His companionship enjoy,
Don't forget—he's just a boy.

Boston Baked Beans

Soak beans overnight. In the morning, parboil them for 10 minutes with a teaspoon of baking soda. Then run cold water through the beans in a colander or strainer.

Dice rind of salt pork into 1-inch squares, then cut in half. Put half on the bottom of a 2-quart bean pot with the whole onion. Put the beans in the pot. Put the rest of the pork on top.

Mix sugar, molasses, mustard, salt, and pepper with hot water. Pour over beans. Put in 300-degree oven for 6 hours.

"You can't let the pot just set in the oven," explains Chef Edward. "You have got to add water as necessary to keep the beans moist. And you can't be impatient and add too much water at a time and flood the beans."

Edward produces his Boston baked beans under the watchful eye of Albert Savage, who has been the head chef at Durgin-Park for the past thirty-five years. Albert is probably the world's leading specialist in Yankee cookery. He himself is an old Yankee who was born in Lithuania. He has one assistant who is a Bulgarian Yankee and another who is a Polish Yankee. "The chief difference between Yankee cooking and most other types of cooking is that we make our food taste like what it's supposed to be," says Albert. "In other kinds of cooking, chefs seem determined to make

2 pounds California pea beans

1 teaspoon baking soda

1 pound salt pork

1 medium onion

8 tablespoons sugar

2/3 cup molasses

2 teaspoons dry mustard

4 teaspoons salt

1/2 teaspoon pepper

Hot water to cover beans

the food taste like something else."

~❧ YIELD ❧~

Serves 10

Tea Cake, Blueberry Cake, and Corn Bread

TEA CAKE

Mix sugar with beaten eggs. Sift flour, baking powder, and salt together. Add melted butter and milk. Beat up quickly and bake in large, buttered pan in a very hot oven. This makes one large pan, or 21 squares.

BLUEBERRY CAKE

Add one cup blueberries last.

CORN BREAD

Substitute one cup granulated yellow cornmeal for one of the three cups of flour.

YIELD

About 21 squares

3/4 cup sugar

2 eggs, beaten

3 cups flour

1 tablespoon baking powder

3/4 teaspoon salt

1 tablespoon butter, melted

1 1/2 cups milk

EMERSON INN
BY THE SEA
Rockport

The temperance movement had much to do with the birth of Emerson Inn by the Sea. Back in 1856, William Norwood ran a very popular tavern in Pigeon Cove near the present post office. Several of the town's women were quite involved with the campaign to eradicate alcohol from every part of their community. Hannah Jumper and two hundred townswomen launched a raid that destroyed all of the alcoholic spirits in Rockport, including those at Norwood's tavern.

Unable to resurrect his tavern business, Norwood turned to the summer vacation trade, which was just beginning to discover Rockport. He and his wife began operating the Pigeon Cove House, an inn "in a pleasant situation" when Granite Street was still a dry and dusty road along the Atlantic coast. It was well suited for the carriage trade of the day.

The natural beauty of Pigeon Cove drew visitors from as far away as New York and it became a popular summer resort for clergy, essayists, and poets. The Norwoods enlarged their house to become "the building of many gables" to accommodate the number of summer guests, which often included families. After William Norwood's death, Mrs. Norwood not only ran the inn on her own but also received wide public approval, "winning respect and commendation . . . from all quarters of the land."

In late 1866, Mrs. Norwood sold the inn to Mrs. Robinson for $9,000. In 1871, Mrs. Robinson decided to move the building to the corner of Philips Avenue and Green Street, its present site. The building soon became a rooming house run by the McGuire family until 1911. Sometime later, after a year and a half of extensive renovations, the inn was reopened as the Hotel Edward. It was advertised as a "luxurious, modern hotel . . . that promised private dining rooms for 'automobile parties,' a chauffeur hall, and a fireproof garage for 30 cars."

Automobile parties were common in those days. Guests would be invited to take a drive, usually in an open-air car complete with goggles for each passenger; they would later enjoy an evening of dinner and entertainment before retiring for the night. Hotel Edward wanted to attract guests wealthy enough to really need a "fireproof garage," which here was the building in front of the pool.

51

The Edward soon gained a reputation as the finest of summer resorts. It is believed that Henry David Thoreau brought Ralph Waldo Emerson to Cape Ann for a hike along the Atlantic coast. They stopped for morning tea in Folly Cove and afternoon tea in Pigeon Cove. Emerson quickly fell in love with Pigeon Cove, and for the next few summers, he brought his family there to vacation. Emerson found inspiration along the rocky coast, which is apparent in his poetry.

Hotel Edward continued to be a grand attraction for guests from all over. It was considered very fashionable and modern, receiving high accolades for "sterling" service. The inn had the first telephones in the "cove," even before anyone else within calling distance owned one. They also had the first telegraph and the first gas, then electric, lights. Hotel Edward always tried to stay a step ahead of any competition.

Tourism was still growing in 1930, and the inn added the area from the dining room on toward the south. In 1964 the Wemyss family bought the inn and reopened it in 1965 as the Ralph Waldo Emerson Inn, renaming it after the inn's most celebrated guest. In 1998, the inn began a new chapter in its history when Mr. and Mrs. Coates purchased the property. What had been informally known as the Emerson Inn took on the formal name of Emerson Inn by the Sea.

The Coates had fallen in love with this beautiful old building and the breathtaking spot it occupies beside the Atlantic Ocean. Their vision of the future includes the restoration and preservation of the inn's former splendor, combined with Pigeon Cove's unique charm and an absolute dedication to award-winning service, known to all "quarters of the land." History came full circle in July 2005 when the inn was offered Rockport's first liquor license since 1933. The original allure of an inn overlooking the Atlantic Ocean still remains.

"Dinner, a time when . . . one should eat wisely but not too well, and talk well but not too wisely."

—W. Somerset Maugham

Emerson Inn by the Sea
1 Cathedral Avenue
Rockport, MA 01966
(978) 546-6321
(800) 964-5550

12 two-ounce butter croissants

1 quart heavy cream

1 cup sugar, granulated

1 Tahitian vanilla bean,
    split and scraped

1 1/2 pounds dark chocolate
    (good-quality 64 percent
    cocoa or above)

12 whole eggs

Chocolate Croissant Bread Pudding

Dice croissants into 3/4-inch cubes and set aside in large mixing bowl.

Heat cream, sugar, and vanilla over medium heat just to scald cream and dissolve sugar.

Coarsely chop chocolate and add to cream mixture. Stir to dissolve.

Add eggs to chocolate cream and whisk until smooth.

Strain through a fine-mesh sieve into a bowl with the croissants.

Mix croissants and chocolate custard by hand, careful not to break up croissants. Allow to soak for 10 minutes.

Transfer to a greased 9" × 12" pan. Place inside another pan with a water bath.

Cover pan with aluminum foil and bake at 325 degrees for approximately 60 minutes, or until bread pudding is set in the center.

YIELD

Serves 12

Maine Blueberry-Ginger Gastrique

Combine sugar, lemon juice, and water in a medium saucepan over medium heat. Allow to become a light caramel without stirring.

Add rice wine vinegar, ginger, and blueberries to caramel. Stir once, bring to a boil, and then reduce to a simmer for 30 minutes.

This sauce can top just about anything. Serve warm or cold on cheesecakes, ice cream, waffles, or my favorite—on top of grilled wild salmon.

YIELD

Serves 8

1/2 cup sugar, granulated

1 teaspoon lemon juice, fresh

1 teaspoon water

1 tablespoon rice wine vinegar

1 tablespoon ginger, fresh, minced fine

2 pints Maine blueberries

1 can sweetened condensed milk,
14 ounces

1 gallon water

1 quart 2 percent milk

12 egg yolks

1/2 teaspoon cinnamon

1 teaspoon vanilla extract

Dulce De Leche Pot De Crème

Bring the water to a boil, remove label from can, and drop can into water. Boil 3 hours, remove, and allow to cool overnight.

In a medium mixing bowl, add the chilled sweetened condensed milk (dulce de leche), milk, eggs, cinnamon, and vanilla. Whisk until all is incorporated.

Place 8 four-ounce soufflé cups in a hot-water bath, then distribute custard batter evenly into the cups.

Cover with aluminum foil and bake at 325 degrees for 45 minutes.

Carefully remove cups from water bath and place them on a baking sheet. Chill for at least 4 hours.

Optional: Serve with crusty baguette and whipped cream or just enjoy on its own.

YIELD

Serves 8

THE FAIRMONT COPLEY PLAZA BOSTON

Boston

Since its opening in 1912, the Fairmont Copley Plaza Boston has stood as a symbol of the city's rich culture, history, and hospitality. Located in the historic Back Bay, the hotel stands alongside the Boston Public Library, Trinity Church, and Hancock Tower, as the architectural landmarks of Copley Square.

Constructed on the original site of the Museum of Fine Arts, the Fairmont Copley Plaza Boston was designed by Henry Janeway Hardenbergh, who also designed the Plaza in New York. The sister hotels share the same double *P* insignia seen throughout both properties.

The hotel's Oval Room, considered one of the most beautiful rooms in Boston, features a realistic sky-and-cloud ceiling mural. Legend has it that when John Singer Sargent was painting the murals at the Boston Public Library, he would often come to the hotel and watch the artisans paint the Oval Room's mural as he enjoyed his lunch. When the artisans asked Sargent to add his touch to the mural, he mounted the scaffolding and painted an angel.

Sargent's angel graced the ceiling for over thirty years until the mural was painted over during renovations in the 1940s. Today, Sargent's angel is considered the invisible guardian of the Oval Room.

Nearly every U.S. president since Taft has stayed at the Fairmont Copley Plaza. Foreign dignitaries, royalty, and countless celebrities have also graced the Boston hotel. In addition, the Fairmont Copley Plaza has been featured in several major motion pictures, including *The Firm* and *Blown Away*.

Today, the Fairmont Copley Plaza celebrates the completion of a $34 million renovation and restoration, which included all of the guest rooms, suites, and meeting spaces and the addition of Fairmont Gold. As part of the renovation, the Fairmont Copley Plaza has added eight suites themed around Boston's rich culture and history. The cultural partners for this project are the John F. Kennedy Library and Museum, the Boston Symphony Orchestra, the Museum of Fine Arts, the

Boston Public Library, the Museum of Science, the Boston Pops, the Freedom Trail, and the Sports Museum. Working with curators and archivists from these organizations, the suites feature artwork and memorabilia designed to give guests an authentic Boston experience.

"I feel a recipe is only a theme, which an intelligent cook can play each time with a variation."

—Madame Benoit

The Fairmont Copley Plaza Boston
138 St. James Avenue
Boston, MA 02116
(617) 867-8574

New England Clam Chowder

In a large pot, combine all the broth ingredients and bring to a boil. Add clams to the broth and cook until the clams open up. Remove clams from the broth and, when cold enough to handle, remove the clam meat from the shells. Cut the meat in half. Strain the broth and reserve.

In the same pot, render the bacon. Add the onions and thyme and cook for a few minutes. Add the celery and cook for a few minutes. Add the broth and bring to a boil. Add the potatoes.

When the potatoes are fully cooked, add the cream and bring to a boil. Add the chopped clams and torn celery leaves. Bring to a boil. Season with salt and pepper. Add lemon juice and serve immediately. Serve with oyster crackers.

YIELD

Serves 6

BROTH

1 tablespoon whole peppercorns

1 bay leaf

1 cup celery, chopped

1 cup Spanish onions, chopped

1 quart white wine

1 quart water

CHOWDER

10 cherry stone clams, well washed

1 cup cob-smoked bacon, diced small

1 cup Spanish onions, diced

1 tablespoon fresh thyme leaves

1 stalk celery, peeled and sliced (save leaves)

2 large Idaho potatoes, peeled and diced into 1/2-inch cubes

1 cup heavy cream

Salt and pepper to taste

1 tablespoon fresh-squeezed lemon juice

Oyster crackers

 *58*

4 tablespoons clarified butter or 2 tablespoons butter mixed with 2 tablespoons canola oil

4 ten-ounce Buffalo tenderloin steaks

Kosher salt to taste

8 tablespoons freshly ground black pepper (not too fine)

1/2 cup cognac

1/2 cup veal stock or beef stock mixed with 1 cup hot water

1 1/2 cups heavy cream

Buffalo Au Poivre

Preheat oven to 350 degrees. Heat sauté pan and add the clarified butter or butter mixed with oil.

Season steaks on each side with salt and 4 tablespoons of the pepper. Make sure you press the salt and pepper firmly into the steaks with your hand. When the butter is hot, place the steaks into the sauté pan and cook until each side is golden brown. Transfer steaks to an oven-safe dish and finish in the oven until cooked to desired temperature.

Discard the fat from the sauté pan and return the pan to the heat. Add the rest of the pepper and the cognac. Be careful as the cognac can catch on fire. Wait until there are no more flames and add the stock and cream. Cook until the sauce starts to thicken. The cooking time will vary depending on the quality of the stock. Reduce the sauce until it coats the back of a spoon.

Salt to taste and pour over the steaks. Serve immediately.

YIELD

Serves 4

Boston Cream Pie

Fairmont Copley Plaza Style

CAKE

Preheat oven to 350 degrees. Butter and flour a 10-inch cake pan. In a mixer, cream butter and sugar until very light and fluffy. Whip in the honey. With mixer set at moderate speed, add eggs one at a time, allowing each to be fully incorporated before adding the next. In a separate bowl, sift together flour, baking powder, and salt. In another bowl, combine milk and vanilla. Alternate adding dry and wet ingredients in 2–3 batches, finishing with dry. Transfer to a cake pan.

Bake 50–60 minutes. Test with skewer (skewer should come out clean). Cool on wire rack 10–15 minutes before unmolding. Place in fridge for a few hours. When very cold, cut cake into three even slices. Brush cake slices evenly with rum.

CREAM FILLING

Combine milk and split vanilla bean in a sauce pot. Bring to a boil. Cream sugar, cornstarch, salt, and eggs in a mixer until mixture starts to turn white. Pour hot milk into sugar mixture while stirring. Put back into sauce pot and cook over medium heat, stirring constantly, until mixture starts to thicken and come to a boil. Remove vanilla bean and add rum. Cool down completely before using.

CAKE

2 1/2 sticks unsalted butter, softened

1 cup sugar

1 cup honey

4 large eggs

3 cups all-purpose flour

2 teaspoons baking powder

1/2 teaspoon salt

1 cup milk

2 teaspoons vanilla extract

2 ounces rum

CREAM FILLING

1 quart milk

1 vanilla bean

1/2 pound sugar

2 1/2 ounces cornstarch

Pinch of salt

3 eggs

2 ounces rum

White chocolate shavings for garnish

ASSEMBLY

Spread cream evenly with a spatula onto the two bottom slices of cake. Stack cake slices, putting no cream on the top one. Right before serving, cut a nice wedge, place on a plate, and pour hot chocolate sauce all over it. Garnish with some white chocolate shavings.

YIELD

1 ten-inch cake

HAMPSHIRE HOUSE
Boston

Most everyone with a television knows *Cheers*, where Kelsey Grammer, John Ratzenberger, Woody Harrelson, Kirstie Alley, and friends hung out for more than a decade of hilarious comedy. And in *Cheers*, as the refrain goes, everybody knows your name to be Dr. Frasier Crane, Cliff Clavin, Woody Boyd, and Rebecca Howe, among others. Only die-hard fans of the show and quite a few travelers to Boston know that the sitcom *Cheers* is patterned after a real bar in town called the Bull & Finch Pub. It is there today for everyone to see. But even most die-hards are unaware that the bar that inspired the setting for *Cheers* is in a building known as the Hampshire House.

The façade of the Hampshire House as the building that is home to *Cheers* is recognizable to millions of sitcom viewers, even if the name is not. The building's history is even less well-known. It was built in 1910 as a private residence for prominent Bostonians Bayard and Ruth Thayer. Society architect Ogden Codman designed and constructed this five-story Georgian Revival townhouse with an eye-popping budget. The home was lavished with Italian marble, carved oak paneling, crystal chandeliers, and tall Palladian windows.

Those windows offer a glimpse of both the Victorian elegance of the Boston Public Garden and the social world of Boston's elite. The address at 84 Beacon Street became one of the most desirable destinations in the city. It was top hats and tails and silk and satin for every event. Every one of Boston's socially aware Brahmins came for a night or more of elegant revelry.

The Hampshire House did not acquire its name until the Thayer family sold the building during World War II. Leased to the owners of the Lincolnshire Hotel on Charles Street, it then became a small, private luxury hotel. Recognizing our major ally in the war, the new owners dubbed the mansion the Hampshire House (both Lincolnshire and Hampshire are English counties).

Upon being converted to a hotel, the mansion required some fundamental changes. The lower floor was converted into a restaurant and cocktail lounge to support the clientele. The second floor was a library, and all the upper floors were made into suites for guests. The second-floor library became a popular location for private events, weddings, and dinners because of the extraordinary location and the magnificent views of the Boston Public Garden.

In 1969, Thomas A. Kershaw bought the building. He and a partner immediately set about converting the downstairs into an authentic English-style pub in recognition of the countryside for

which the building is named. Of course, they hoped to be successful, but even Kershaw would probably admit that they did not expect the notoriety they ultimately received.

The Bull & Finch Pub was patterned after a real English pub. Following an extensive research trip through the English countryside, Tom's partner, Jack Veasy, had a small pub constructed "over there" and then shipped to Boston. English craftsmen were also brought over to assemble the various parts, which can now be seen on your next visit to Boston.

The one detail that they overlooked was the door for the pub. In solving this problem, they eventually converted the back door into a front door. A great many scenes in the *Cheers* sitcom show this door, but of course Hollywood doesn't always get it right. Unlike the Bull & Finch Pub, the door of the show set opens inward—a direct violation of Boston's fire code, which requires that all doors open outward.

Since syndication of the television show in many foreign lands and languages, tourists come from across the world exploring the origin of *Cheers*. They can't help but marvel when they happen upon the grand staircase in the lobby of the Hampshire House.

The mansion is often used for private events, but every so often the doors are open to the public. Brunches are held in the library almost every Sunday from September to June. Special holiday brunches and dinners are held on the second and third floors.

Many would call the library Melville's, the upscale restaurant depicted in the TV show, located directly upstairs from the famous bar. Comedy often arose from the conflict between the restaurant's management, which found the bar's clientele decidedly uncouth, while Sam Malone, who owned *Cheers*, regarded the restaurant as snobbish. Even today, Melville's, which shares the name of Tom Kershaw's father, serves great food in this turn-of-the-century mansion located on historic Beacon Hill.

Hampshire House
84 Beacon Street
Boston, MA 02108
(617) 227-9600

Punch Romaine

Champagne and lemon ice

In blender, combine crushed ice, simple syrup, champagne, white wine, orange juice, and lemon juice. Blend until well combined.

Spoon mixture into individual dessert cups. Drizzle with white rum (if using) and garnish with a sliver of orange peel. Serve immediately.

❧ YIELD ❧

Serves 8

6 cups crushed ice

1 cup simple syrup

2 cups champagne or sparkling wine

1 cup white wine

1/3 cup freshly squeezed orange juice

2 tablespoons lemon juice

2 tablespoons white rum (optional)

Orange peel, slivered

BOAR

1 six- to eight-pound boar leg
(hind leg)

1 tablespoon olive oil

1 tablespoon cracked black
pepper

2 tablespoons balsamic vinegar

2 tablespoons garlic, chopped

Sprig rosemary, chopped

1 tablespoon garlic mustard

1/2 tablespoon coarse sea salt

RELISH

1 pound prune plums, fresh
pitted and diced

1/2 red onion, chopped

1 red pepper, diced

1 tablespoon raspberry vinegar

1/2 tablespoon balsamic vinegar

1 tablespoon olive oil

1 tablespoon brown sugar

Cayenne, salt, and freshly ground
pepper to taste

1 sprig flat-leaf parsley

Wild Boar Leg with Prune Plum Relish

Wild boar is available at specialty butchers and food shops. It is bred on many farms and ranches locally and throughout the United States. It is much leaner than domestic pork, and the meat is redder. It makes a welcome change for beef lovers. If you have a rotisserie available, this recipe is made for it.

BOAR

Rub all ingredients on leg.

Place on roasting tray and roast in oven, turning occasionally, for 30 minutes at 400 degrees. Remove from oven and let stand covered in warm area for 15 minutes before slicing and serving with relish.

RELISH

Mix all ingredients and let stand for 4–6 hours. This relish tastes even better the next day after refrigerating overnight.

YIELD

Serves 6

Sautéed Beet Greens and Caramelized Shallots

In a large sauté pan, sauté shallots until golden.

Add brown sugar and heat until caramelized.

Add carrots, peppers, and beet greens and toss for a couple of seconds. Add dressing.

Arrange on a plate with the peppered goat cheese.

Garnish with fresh herbs of choice and serve immediately.

Whisk dressing ingredients in a bowl and toss lightly over salad.

YIELD

Serves 4

2 shallots, sliced

1 tablespoon brown sugar

1 cup each carrots and peppers, diced

1 bunch young beet greens

1 goat-cheese log cut in slices and covered in cracked black pepper

DRESSING

2 ounces malt vinegar

4 ounces extra virgin olive oil

Sprinkling of fresh thyme

1 tablespoon pommery mustard

Salt to taste

HOTEL NORTHAMPTON

Northampton

As guests wander through the Hotel Northampton, the integral elements that its builder, Lewis Wiggins, incorporated in the design are captivating. Lewis had an uncanny interest in, and love of, Colonial Revival period pieces, and those same antiques that he lovingly collected still grace the hotel, lobby, and tavern, as they did in 1927.

His vast collection grew to such enormity that within ten years, Lewis actually employed a full-time curator with full knowledge of antiques and a staff of fifteen to enhance the collection. He employed two of his staff solely to mingle with the guests and impart their enthusiasm for history and antiques so that guests left with a true sense of relaxation, a love of history, and a firm grasp of the period.

Wiggins had a passion for fine American food, and in search of a way to further entertain his guests, he purchased the Moriarity Building located next door to the hotel. His determination to construct an actual replica of an Early American tavern was delightful. Over 140 years before, in 1786, Benjamin Wiggins, a direct ancestor of Lewis, ran the Wiggins Tavern in Hopkinton, New Hampshire. Benjamin had earned a fine reputation for serving great fare and spirits in the region. Thus, Lewis decided to move the old tavern to the hotel. He had the brick hearths, hand-hewn beams, and finely carved paneling totally reconstructed. His attention to detail was uncanny. He continued to collect antiques and also brought those from the original tavern. Today, the Wiggins Tavern is much the same as it appeared over two hundred years ago.

Eleanor Roosevelt, Jenny Lind, Herbert Hoover, Calvin Coolidge, Dwight Eisenhower, John F. Kennedy, and Richard Nixon have all enjoyed meals and conversation at the tavern. During World War II, the U.S. Navy Waves were billeted at Smith College and enjoyed three square meals each day at the tavern. One of the Waves said that there were two great things about being stationed at Northampton: "You survived the war, and you got to eat at Wiggins Tavern."

"All happiness depends on a leisurely breakfast."

—John Gunther

Hotel Northampton
36 King Street
Northampton, MA 01060
(800) 547-3529

 *68*

BATTER

1/2 cup butter, softened

1 1/3 cups granulated sugar

2 eggs

2 1/4 cups all-purpose flour

1 teaspoon baking powder

1/2 teaspoon salt

1 cup milk

2 cups fresh or frozen blueberries

6 ounces cream cheese, cubed

TOPPING

4 tablespoons all-purpose flour

4 tablespoons granulated sugar

2 tablespoons butter

Blueberry Coffee Cake

In a large mixing bowl, cream softened butter and sugar. Beat in eggs.

In a separate bowl, combine 2 cups flour, baking powder, and salt. Gradually add to creamed mixture alternately with 1 cup of milk.

Toss blueberries with remaining flour. Stir blueberries and cream cheese cubes into creamed mixture (batter will be thick). Transfer to a greased Bundt pan.

In a mixing bowl, combine 4 tablespoons flour and 4 tablespoons granulated sugar. Cut in 2 tablespoons butter until crumbly. Sprinkle over batter.

Bake at 325 degrees for 40–45 minutes, or until toothpick inserted near the center comes out clean. Cool on wire rack.

YIELD

Serves 10–12

Wiggins Tavern
Pan-Seared Salmon

Heat oil in sauté pan until oil is very hot but not smoking. Salt and pepper both sides of salmon fillet, placing salmon in pan. Keep heat on medium, allowing salmon to brown. Turn with tongs (without breaking) and brown other side.

Add garlic and sun-dried tomatoes to pan and sauté lightly. Deglaze in pan with white wine, reducing by half. Add vegetable stock and allow to reduce again by half. After reduction, salmon will be cooked. Add whole butter to give sheen to sauce.

Remove salmon with spatula and pour sauce over the top.

This dish can be served over pasta or rice. The sauce can also be further reduced and served as a glaze.

YIELD
Serves 2

2 tablespoons olive oil

Salt and pepper

1 ten-ounce salmon fillet, skinless

1 teaspoon garlic, chopped

2 tablespoons puréed sun-dried tomatoes (soak in water overnight, drain, and lightly pulse in food processor)

1/2 cup white wine

1 cup vegetable stock

1 tablespoon butter (cold)

18 egg yolks

2 cups powdered sugar

1 cup maple syrup

6 cups heavy cream

Maple Crème Brûlée

Whisk egg yolks and sugar together until combined. Add maple syrup and whisk well. Add heavy cream to egg mixture.

Pour into pitcher and skim foam off the top of the mixture.

Pour mixture into 18 ramekins and place ramekins in a hot-water bath in 2-inch-deep pans.

Cover with foil and bake at 275 degrees for 1 hour, or until centers are almost set.

Take off foil and finish cooking for another 5–10 minutes.

Let cool in pans and then refrigerate.

YIELD

18

JURYS
BOSTON HOTEL
Boston

It should come as no surprise to many people that the most Irish city in America is Boston, Massachusetts. Knowing this will help you understand why a Dublin, Ireland–based company would want to own and operate an exclusive hotel in Boston. Jurys Doyle Hotel Group has created a four-star attraction in the Jurys Boston Hotel. And they did it by renovating a historic building.

In 1925, the Boston police headquarters was relocated to 350 Stuart Street. Although that may sound like a very long time ago, but the truth is that this was the department's third headquarters, and it has already moved on from there.

Boston has the oldest police department in the country. The city's first actual community safety activity really began in 1635 when it established a formal night watch. The watchmen were not called "police" then, but they performed the same function. Thus, the people of Boston had the first paid, professional public-safety unit in America.

It was not until 1788 that the word "police" appeared in Boston when the town designated the office of inspector of police. At this point, the police unit, being relatively small, was headquartered in the city hall.

In 1883, the general court passed a bill allowing the city of Boston to appoint police officers. The department was structured after the model developed by Sir Robert Peele for the London police force. All city functions and responsibilities had grown so large at this point that the police department moved out of city hall to a new headquarters at 37 Pemberton Square.

By 1925, the department had grown even more, reflecting the growth of the city of Boston, necessitating the move to a new structure at the corner of Stuart and Berkeley streets. This new headquarters served the department well for many years, until 1997, when the department moved into its current state-of-the-art facility at One Schroeder Plaza.

Following the departure of the police headquarters and extensive renovations by the Jurys Doyle Hotel Group, the Jurys Boston Hotel was born. Opening in July 2004, the hotel offers 225 guest rooms and three executive suites.

Boston at one point had an Irish population of more than 70 percent, but this number has declined drastically in the past two centuries. However, the heritage remains. The chic Stanhope Grille

is a cosmopolitan restaurant and outdoor patio serving hearty authentic Irish breakfasts, freshly prepared lunches, and a full dinner menu. Cuffs—an Irish Bar—features innovative furnishings and seating groups and exotic finishes of rosewood, leather, steel, and stone, creating an aura of conviviality and good Irish cheer.

Jurys Boston Hotel offers warm Irish hospitality coupled with modern luxury in a truly historic setting.

Jurys Boston Hotel
350 Stuart Street
Back Bay
Boston, MA 02116
(617) 532-3821

Lobster Bisque

Heat oil in the skillet. Add lobster heads and onions, celery, and carrots.

Brown the veggies. Then add tomato paste and cook until it is almost burnt.

Add sherry and brandy and reduce.

Add heavy cream, salt, and pepper and simmer for 1 hour.

❧ YIELD ❧

Serves 24

1 cup olive oil

20 lobster heads

4 onions

1 bunch celery

4 carrots

4 ounces tomato paste

3 cups sherry

3 cups brandy

2 cups heavy cream

Salt and pepper to taste

2 1/2 cups water

1 cup lemon juice

1 1/2 cups sugar

Zest of 1 lemon

1/4 cup Limoncello

Limoncello Sorbet

Combine water, lemon juice, and sugar in a pot. Bring to boil until the sugar is dissolved. Remove from the heat.

Add the lemon zest and leave still for 10 minutes.

Strain the zest, add limoncello, and put through the ice-cream machine.

YIELD

Serves 20

THE LENOX HOTEL
Boston

⸻

In 1900, the famous hotelier Lucias Boomer, best known as the owner of New York's Waldorf-Astoria, began work on what was to be the most luxurious hotel in New England. It took eight months and $1.1 million to complete the Lenox, which was the tallest building in the city of Boston at the time. Set in the heart of the Back Bay, the Lenox created a new standard for quality hotels in New England.

Since that time, the Lenox has become a home-away-from-home for luminaries in entertainment, business, sports, and the arts. Boston society has long regarded the Lenox as a popular gathering place for any type of social event.

Since 1963, the Saunders family, through the Saunders Hotel Group, has been at the helm of the Lenox. In the business for three generations, they are widely known for gracious hospitality, innovation, and environmental leadership. They have been responsible for a series of meticulous restorations, including one in 2003 that earned worldwide accolades for historic preservation and design.

The Saunders Hotel Group also owns or operates several other distinctive properties, including the charming Copley Square Hotel, and is particularly conscious of the environment. The Lenox Hotel offers such unique features a "cool room," which guarantees guests that their stay will have no negative effect on global warming.

While the cool room is part of their climate-neutral accommodations, they also use low-flow bathroom fixtures, an ionizing system in their swimming pools that eliminates chlorine, attractive dispensers rather than throw-away plastic bottles for their very high-quality shampoo, soap, and lotion, closed-loop cooling towers, and water-conserving, air-cooled equipment. They go out of their way to ensure that every employee lives in Boston, and they make sure that service to the guests meets the very high standards set when the Lenox Hotel first opened. To reward the staff for the excellence of service to guests, the Lenox provides the child or grandchild of every employee with a four-year scholarship worth $120,000 at Newbury College's Roger A. Saunders School of Hotel & Restaurant Management.

 *76*

An unwavering commitment to total guest comfort and innovation, as well as a strong sense of community responsibility, characterize the Saunders family's management approach. The Lenox's industry-leading environmental efforts have received numerous prestigious awards for pioneering luxury within ecotourism, including a gold medal from President George H. W. Bush in 1992.

The Lenox Hotel
61 Exeter Street at Boylston
Boston, MA 02116
(617) 536-5300

Awesome Pound Cake

POUND CAKE

Sift together flour, salt, baking soda, and baking powder.

Cream the butter and sugar.

Slowly add the eggs.

Add the buttermilk and vanilla extract.

Bake in 3 loaf pans at 325 degrees for 70–80 minutes.

Allow to cool at room temp.

THREE-BERRY COMPOTE

Actually, you can use any combination of berries you like. The later it gets into the season, you can throw some sliced stone fruits into the mix as well.

Mix all ingredients together and allow to sit for a few hours at room temperature.

PLATING

Slice a nice slab of pound cake, put a generous ladle of berry compote over the top, garnish with fresh whipped cream, mint sprig, and powdered sugar.

YIELD

Makes 3 loaves

POUND CAKE

6 cups cake flour

1/2 teaspoon salt

1/2 teaspoon baking soda

1 teaspoon baking powder

2 pounds butter

2 pounds sugar

12 eggs

1 cup buttermilk

1/8 cup vanilla extract

THREE-BERRY COMPOTE

1/2 cup strawberries, sliced

1/2 cup blueberries

1/2 cup blackberries

Juice and zest of 1/2 lemon

Juice and zest of 1/2 orange

1/4 cup granulated sugar

5 pounds small new potatoes

1 pound apple-smoked bacon

1 teaspoon salad oil

1 cup yellow onion, diced small

1/2 cup apple cider vinegar

3/4 cup brown sugar

1 cup salad oil

1/4 cup Dijon mustard

1/4 cup parsley, chopped

1 bunch green onion, slivered

2 tablespoons Worcestershire
    sauce

Cracked black pepper as needed

Salt as needed

Fathman Family German Potato Salad

Blanch the potatoes in their jackets and cut into quarters while still warm.

Cut the bacon into tasty bits. Cook in 1 teaspoon of salad oil until nice and crispy. Drain off the bacon fat.

Cook the onions until well caramelized over moderate heat.

Mix potatoes, bacon, and onions with vinegar, brown sugar, salad oil, mustard, parsley, green onion, Worcestershire sauce, pepper, and salt. Serve warm or at room temperature.

YIELD

Serves 15–20

Grilled Flank Steak with Infused Rum-Ginger Glaze

Mix all ingredients for the dry rub together and cover the flank steak with it. Refrigerate and allow to sit for 1 to 2 days.

Mix all ingredients for the glaze together and, on low to moderate heat, reduce by 2/3 until nice and syrupy.

Grill the meat to medium rare over a hot hardwood charcoal, approximately 3–4 minutes per side. Dredge the meat in the glaze and allow the meat to rest for approximately 4 minutes.

Before serving, toss the flank back onto the hottest part of the grill to get some char and caramelization from the sugars in the glaze, 30 seconds on each side. Slice the flank on the bias as thinly as possible.

Serve the meat with a side of the glaze or some ice cold beer.

YIELD
Serves 4

2 flank steaks

DRY RUB

1 teaspoon salt

1 tablespoon black pepper

1/4 teaspoon cinnamon, ground

1/4 teaspoon allspice, ground

1 tablespoon granulated sugar

1 teaspoon chili powder

1/4 teaspoon cumin, ground

1 teaspoon dried thyme

DIABOLIQUE-INFUSED RUM GLAZE

1 1/2 cup diabolique rum

1/2 cup brown sugar

1/2 cup molasses

1/2 cup red wine vinegar

1 tablespoon sambal olek

1 small cinnamon stick

1 tablespoon Dijon mustard

1 tablespoon sweet soy sauce

5–8 ears corn (depending on how much you like corn)

1 cup Parmesan cheese, grated

GARLIC BUTTER

1 pound unsalted butter

1/4 cup garlic, minced

Juice of 1 lemon

Zest of 1 lemon

1/4 cup parsley, chopped

Salt and pepper as needed

Grilled Corn with Garlic Butter and Parmesan Cheese

Clean the corn by peeling off the husks; leave as many attached to the corn as possible. Tie the husks off with butcher's twine to provide a handle for eating the corn without getting all buttery.

Blanch the corn in boiling salted water.

Allow the butter to come to room temperature and mix all of the garlic butter ingredients together. This simple compound butter can be made a few days ahead of time and kept in the fridge. Don't worry if you have some left over; its great for finishing sauces, dressing veggies, or making garlic bread.

Grill the corn (preferably over medium-heat hardwood charcoal), lavishly brush with garlic butter, and roll in the Parmesan cheese.

YIELD

Serves 5–8

LONGFELLOW'S WAYSIDE INN

Sudbury

Longfellow's Wayside Inn, the oldest operating inn in the country, was immortalized by Henry Wadsworth Longfellow in 1863 in *Tales of a Wayside Inn*:

> The scroll reads, "By the name of Howe."
> And over this, no longer bright,
> Though glimmering with a latent light,
> Was hung the sword his grandsire bore
> In the rebellious days of yore,
> Down there at Concord in the fight.

Longfellow's Wayside Inn was originally named Howe's Tavern from 1716 to 1861. The original innkeeper, David Howe, operated a "house of entertainment" along the old Boston Post Road in the same spot the Wayside Inn stands today. Before it was an inn, it was a home, so at least part of the structure was actually built prior to 1716.

David and Hebzibah Howe's original home was quite different from the Wayside Inn's rambling structure. It was typical by eighteenth-century standards, having just two rooms, one over the other. They raised five children in this house, which is probably why David doubled its size, adding two more rooms by the time he received a license to operate an inn in 1716. The size of the Howe's home and business continued to grow as each subsequent innkeeper made additions and improvements to this colonial landmark.

The son and grandson of innkeepers, David Howe knew he would be successful due to the busy coach traffic to and from the cities of Boston and Worcester. In 1746, the fourth generation of innkeepers took over when he passed the family business to his son, Ezekiel. A lieutenant colonel during the Revolutionary War, Ezekiel led the Sudbury Minute and Militia to Concord Center on that fateful day, April 19, 1775, that began the American Revolution.

Ezekiel prospered as an innkeeper, eventually passing the inn to his son, Adam, in 1796, who in turn handed it down to his son, Lyman, in 1830. When Lyman died in 1861 having never married,

the inn was inherited by relatives who ceased operating the Howe home as an overnight accommodation. The hall was occasionally rented out for dances, and itinerant farmers occupied smaller rooms for lengthy stays, but the Howe inn-keeping business would not thrive again until a wool merchant from Malden, Massachusetts, showed new interest in 1897.

Edward Rivers Lemon purchased the inn as "a retreat for literary pilgrims," capitalizing on the interest generated by Henry Longfellow's *Tales of a Wayside Inn*. Longfellow had visited the Howe Tavern in 1862 and wrote his book about a group of fictitious characters that regularly gathered at the old Sudbury Tavern. Lyman Howe was the character featured in *The Landlord's Tale*, in which Longfellow penned the immortal phrase "listen my children and you shall hear, of the midnight ride of Paul Revere." Edward Lemon fully embraced Longfellow and the attention he brought to the old inn. He renamed the old Howe Tavern Longfellow's Wayside Inn and operated it with his wife, Cora, until his death in 1919.

Cora Lemon sold the inn in 1923 to automobile manufacturer Henry Ford, who would eventually have the most visual impact on the property. He moved the one-room Redstone School to the grounds in 1925, built the gristmill in 1929 and the Martha-Mary Chapel in 1940, and acquired some three thousand acres around the inn. He developed a trade school for boys, which operated from 1928 to 1947, and many believe he intended to build the "village site" he eventually created in Dearborn, Michigan, in Sudbury. Henry Ford was the last private owner of the Wayside Inn. Ford created the nonprofit status that the inn operates under today.

The Wayside Inn Archives contain over half a million documents relating to the history of Longfellow's Wayside Inn. Included among the papers are deeds, wills, photographs, news clippings, menus, and inn-keeping records. While the oldest document in the collection dates to 1686, the Wayside Inn Archives also house papers related to late nineteenth- and early twentieth-century business, while the inn was owned and operated by auto magnate Henry Ford.

Longfellow's Wayside Inn
72 Wayside Inn Road
Sudbury, MA 01776
(978) 443-1776
(800) 339-1776

Yankee Pot Roast

In a Dutch oven or tasting pan, brown the roast.

Put stalks of celery, carrots, and onion around meat. Sprinkle roast with salt and peppercorns. Add water. Bring to a boil, cover, and simmer over low heat or in a 350-degree oven for 2 1/2 hours.

Lift out the roast, keeping it warm. Strain the stock, discarding the vegetables. Slice and serve.

YIELD

Serves 12

4–6 pounds bottom round roast (tied)

2 medium celery stalks

2 carrots

1 small onion, sliced

2 teaspoons salt

6 peppercorns or 1 teaspoon ground black pepper

1 quart water

6 cloves

1 medium onion, peeled and sliced in half

2 cups light cream

2 tablespoons butter

2 tablespoons flour

1 pound smoked haddock fillets, sliced

Creamed Finnan Haddie

Stab cloves into half the onion and simmer in the cream for approximately 1/2 hour. In a heavy-bottomed saucepan, melt butter and add flour to form a roux. Strain hot cream into the roux and simmer for about 10 minutes.

Place fish fillets in a casserole dish and cover with the sauce. Bake for 20 minutes at 350 degrees.

YIELD

Serves 2

Lobster Casserole

Sauté onions and celery in oil until cooked. Mix with lobster, butter, sherry, paprika, Parmesan cheese, parsley, and white pepper thoroughly in a large mixing bowl. Set aside to cool.

Place the cooked lobster meat in a buttered casserole dish. Cover with crumbs and melted butter. Bake until browned, approximately 10–15 minutes at 350 degrees.

YIELD

Serves 8

3/4 pounds onions, finely chopped

1/2 celery stalk, finely chopped

4 pounds lobster meat, cooked

4 ounces clarified butter (or cooking oil)

1 1/2 ounces sherry

1/4 ounce paprika

3 ounces grated Parmesan cheese

1 ounce fresh parsley, chopped

Pinch of white pepper

3/4 pound bread crumbs

3/4 pound Ritz crackers, crumbled

1/4 cup butter

OCEAN EDGE RESORT AND CLUB

Brewster

The original house on the site of the Ocean Edge Resort was Fieldstone Hall. It was built in 1890 by Samuel Mayo Nickerson, a prominent local figure with deep New England roots. Born in nearby Chatham, Massachusetts, in 1830, Nickerson was the child of direct descendents of Puritan settlers who landed on the cape in the 1600s. Nickerson left school when he was seventeen and worked his way to Chicago. By 1858, he had established a prosperous career as a distiller of alcohol and high wines. That same year, he married Matilda P. Crosby of Brewster, and the couple gave birth to their only child, Roland, the following year.

In 1863, Samuel's career took a turn toward prominence when he cofounded the First National Bank of Chicago. He became president four years later and held the position for nearly a quarter century before retiring as a multimillionaire by 1891.

The attraction of the Atlantic brought Samuel back to Brewster. Legend says that on one particular morning, he thrust his gold-tipped cane into the ground and decided that a house would be built there for his only son and his family. Fieldstone Hall was erected for Roland, his wife Addie, and their three fortunate children—Roland Jr., Samuel, and Helen—on a forty-eight-acre parcel overlooking the bay. Completed in 1890, the three-story home boasted four chimneys, and the property included a carriage house complete with a stone tower for taking in the expansive coastal views.

When Roland moved his family into Fieldstone Hall, he was a prominent banker in his own right. The estate, said to have been staffed by nearly two dozen servants, was the scene of frequent and lavish parties thrown by the socially and politically prominent Nickersons over the years and attended by such luminaries as President Grover Cleveland.

The era came to an end on May 10, 1906, when Fieldstone Hall was completely destroyed by fire. Only the foundation survived. The local newspaper reported that as Fieldstone "was licked up by flames, Hon. Roland C. Nickerson, sick from heart disease, waved farewell and circled around the scene in his automobile to safety." The fire also claimed the family's wardrobe, rare old china, and a myriad of paintings and books with a value of $500,000, or $497,000 more than was covered by the family's insurance. Devastated by the tragedy, Roland succumbed to his poor health just two weeks later.

It took a year, but the Nickersons rebounded and rebuilt on the original foundation. Style was brought up to date, and Samuel insisted that his daughter-in-law and grandchildren would live in a fireproof house. Fieldstone Hall was rebuilt with steel-reinforced concrete covered by stucco to be nearly conflagration-proof. He also made it much larger.

The new mansion included sixteen bedrooms, each named after a historic U.S. naval commander and all sumptuously outfitted with Italian marble fireplaces, individual bathrooms, and walk-in closets. Italian woodworkers were brought in to create the fine interiors. The main entrance hall boasted an intricately carved oak staircase, while the porte cochere led to a billiards room complete with the heads of Shakespearean characters watching the players. The room also served as a roller-skating arena for the Nickerson children and their friends. Smaller rooms on the third floor were created to house the staff, and an iron cage elevator was installed for ease of mobility between floors. Leaded glass windows and wide terraces overlooking the bay added to the feeling of grandeur. The old carriage house was refaced in stucco to match the new mansion. The work was completed by 1912, the year Samuel's wife, Matilda, died and just two years before Samuel himself passed away.

The mansion remained in the Nickerson family until 1945, when it was sold to the LaSalette religious order. The clerics used it as a seminary and home for wayward boys. Corcoran Jennison purchased the property in 1980 and opened the resort in 1986.

In early 2006, ClubCorp added Ocean Edge Resort and Club on Cape Cod to its club resorts management portfolio, which includes Pinehurst, Barton Creek Resort & Spa, and the Homestead. Today, the mansion and carriage house have been enhanced to befit their historic character.

Yet, the most prominent fixture on the 429-acre property harkens back to the turn of the nineteenth century. It is the mansion, an exquisite and historic Victorian-style manse, that is one of the cape's grandest historical attractions. The mansion is listed on the National Register of Historic Places.

Ocean Edge Resort and Club
2907 Main Street (Route 6A)
Brewster, MA 02631
(508) 896-9000

1 ounce Bacardi rum

1/2 ounce Malibu rum

1/2 ounce Peachtree schnapps

1/4 ounce Blue Curaçao

2 ounces orange juice

2 ounces pineapple juice

Boyle's Delight

Combine all ingredients into a mixing glass. Add ice, stir to chill, and strain into an ice-chilled martini glass. Garnish with a cocktail flower (with a cherry tucked between the wedges of an orange).

YIELD

Serves 1

Chicken with Riesling

Melt 2 tablespoons of the butter in a large skillet. Add the chicken, season with salt and pepper, and cook over moderate heat until slightly browned, about 4 minutes per side.

Add the shallot and cook, stirring, for 1 minute.

Add the cognac and carefully ignite it with a long match. When the flames subside, add the Riesling, cover, and simmer over low heat until the chicken breasts are just cooked, about 25 minutes.

Transfer the breasts to a large plate and cover with foil. Cover and simmer the legs until cooked through, about 10 minutes longer. Transfer to the plate.

Meanwhile, in a medium skillet, melt 2 tablespoons of the butter. Add the mushrooms, season with salt and pepper, and cook over low heat until the liquid evaporates, about 7 minutes. Increase the heat to moderate and cook, stirring until browned, about 3 minutes.

In a bowl, blend the flour and the remaining 1 tablespoon of butter. Stir the cream into the large skillet and bring to a simmer. Gradually whisk the flour paste into the cooking liquid and simmer, whisking, until no floury taste remains, about 3 minutes. Season with salt and pepper.

5 tablespoons unsalted butter

1 three-and-a-half-pound chicken, quartered

Salt and freshly ground pepper

1 large shallot, minced

2 tablespoons cognac

1 cup dry Riesling

6 ounces white mushrooms, sliced 1/4 inch thick

1 tablespoon all-purpose flour

1/3 cup heavy cream

Return the chicken to the skillet, add the mushrooms and briefly reheat.

Serve with noodles, spaetzles, rice, or boiled potatoes.

YIELD

Serves 4

The Mansion Lobster Salad with Avocado and Tarragon Mayonnaise

Chop the cooked lobster meat and set aside while preparing the tarragon mayonnaise.

Combine mayonnaise, olive oil, lemon juice, dill, celery, and tarragon in a mixing bowl.

Fold the lobster meat into the tarragon mayonnaise.

Stuff the quartered avocados with the lobster salad.

Arrange the baby greens on a platter and place the stuffed avocados atop the greens.

Garnish with lemon wedge and fresh sprig of tarragon. Salt and pepper to taste.

YIELD

Serves 4

3 pounds of lobster meat, cooked

2 ripe avocados, pitted and cut into quarters

2 cups baby greens

1 whole lemon, wedged

Salt and pepper to taste

TARRAGON MAYONNAISE

3 cup mayonnaise

1 tablespoon extra virgin olive oil

2 tablespoons lemon juice

2 tablespoons fresh dill, minced

1 cup celery, chopped fine

1 tablespoon fresh tarragon, chopped

1/2 cup green pepper, chopped

1/4 cup onion, chopped

3 tablespoons olive oil

2 cups mayonnaise

1 tablespoon Dijon mustard

1 tablespoon parsley, chopped

2 tablespoons lemon juice

1/2 cup bread crumbs

1 pound jumbo lump crabmeat

Dash of Tabasco sauce

2 two- or three-pound lobsters

1 whole lemon

Parsley sprigs

Drawn butter

Ocean Grille Stuffed Lobster

Sauté green pepper and onion together in olive oil.

In a large bowl, mix mayonnaise, Dijon mustard, chopped parsley, lemon juice, bread crumbs, jumbo lump crabmeat, and dash of Tabasco sauce.

Fold the green pepper and onions into the stuffing mix.

Set the stuffing mix aside.

Split the lobsters down the middle and clean cavities. Crack lobster claws.

Place the crab stuffing mix into the cavity of each lobster.

Bake in oven at 350 degrees for 20 minutes.

Garnish on a large platter with a lemon cut in half, fresh parsley, and drawn butter.

YIELD

Serves 4–6

OLD STURBRIDGE VILLAGE

Sturbridge

The village exists because of the success of one early entrepreneur. George Washington Wells started with a modest central Massachusetts "spectacle shop" in the late 1840s and built it into a major firm by the turn of the century. The American Optical Company of Southbridge, Massachusetts, became a major business success and created substantial wealth for George's sons. Channing M., Albert B. "A. B.," and J. Cheney Wells all followed their father into the business, creating an even more successful enterprise.

These three men all developed a passion for collecting that would ultimately result in the founding of Old Sturbridge Village. On a rainy day in Vermont in 1926, A. B. Wells was unable to play golf with three friends. He coaxed them into joining him instead on an expedition in search of "antiques." He had been a part-time collector, but that afternoon he became obsessed with the ordinary objects of New England's past, which he referred to as "my primitives." From that day forward, he worked to fit his passionate concern for collecting into his busy life as a prominent industrialist.

Channing, the oldest of the brothers and the long-time company president, collected primarily fine furniture. Cheney took up collecting as well. Reserved, precise, and methodical, he began to amass a significant collection of Early American clocks and timepieces. In the 1920s, many of them decorated the American Optical Company's executive offices.

A. B.'s collecting specialized in the manufacturing side of his business. He loved things that had been handmade in the New England countryside, things that were simple and rustic rather than ornate and urbane. Anything ingenious in design, unusual in appearance, or even bizarre was especially prized. He delighted in wooden bowls and painted country furniture, scythes and hay rakes, redware pots and butter churns. He even found a mouse trap with a guillotine-like double deadfall, an example of Wood's Patented Portable Washing Machine, and devices for breaking cheese curd and crushing apples.

Their leisure pursuits took the Wells brothers on a path that would lead to the creation of a major American museum. Ironically, the same course was also being taken by members of other prominent American industrial families. John D. Rockefeller Jr. would create Colonial Williamsburg, Henry

Ford would give rise to Greenfield Village, and Henry Francis DuPont would bring about Winterthur. They were all serious collectors and preservers of the American past.

A. B.'s collection grew through the 1920s. As the collection grew, new rooms were added to his large Southbridge home. By the early 1930s, there were more than forty-five rooms full of New England "primitives" in the Southbridge house, and the question of what to do with this extraordinary profusion of ordinary things could no longer be avoided.

In 1935, A. B., his brothers, other members of the family, and trusted associates incorporated the Wells Historical Museum. A nonprofit educational corporation, the museum took title to the collections and became responsible for their care and public display.

In July 1936, there was a gathering of the Wells family as museum trustees to determine a future course. A. B.'s son, George, suggested that because of the historical value of the many items they had collected, it would be necessary to have a live village with different shops operating to demonstrate the manner in which their ancestors had lived. Thus, the village was to be not simply an outdoor museum but an active outdoor museum with craftsmen and costumed staff as well as houses and artifacts.

Within a week, they had purchased David Wight's old farm in Sturbridge, a tract of some 153 acres. The site was perfect for realizing their plans. It had sloping meadows, wooded hillsides, and a fine location for waterpower along the Quinebaug River. The Wells Historical Museum became the Quinabaug Village Corporation, with the goal to "operate a model village wherein shall be exhibited and carried on for the educational benefit of the public specimens and reproductions of New England architecture and antiquities, the arts, crafts, trades, and callings."

The Center Meetinghouse was moved to the village from the nearby Fiskdale neighborhood. The Baptist Society had traded their old building for an organ for their new house of worship. By 1941, the Fitch House, the Miner Grant Store, and the Richardson House (now the parsonage) were on the common, and the gristmill, a largely reconstructed building housing early machinery, was in operation on the millpond.

World War II halted construction and development, but in 1945, active leadership of the project passed to the next generation. At A. B.'s urging, his daughter-in-law Ruth Wells, George B.'s wife, became acting director of the village, moving the construction work forward with renewed energy.

In 1946, Quinabaug Village, with the approval of town selectmen, became Old Sturbridge Village and in June opened to the public. Admission was $1 per person, and eighty-one visitors toured the village. By 1955, the graceful Salem Towne House from nearby Charlton was under restoration at the opposite end of the common from the meetinghouse. The Fenno House, the Friends Meetinghouse, the Pliny Freeman House, the printing office, and the district school had also become vital parts of the village landscape.

In 1956, fire destroyed the wooden blacksmith shop, sharply demonstrating an occupational hazard for such structures in the nineteenth century. It was soon replaced by the granite-walled shop from Bolton, Massachusetts, that visitors admire today.

After more than sixty years, the village is a very different place in many ways. It has been expanded and refined. It reaches nearly half a million visitors annually, compared to the 5,170 of 1946. As the village has sharpened its concern with historical authenticity, many parts of its landscape now resemble that of David Wight's 1830s farm much more closely. The "live village" has become a national treasure, whose story is of enduring importance to America's collective memory.

Old Sturbridge Village
1 Old Sturbridge Village Road
Sturbridge, MA 01566
(508) 347-3362

Juice of 3 large oranges

2 tablespoons orange rind

3 eggs, well beaten

2 cups cream

1/8 teaspoon cinnamon

1/8 teaspoon nutmeg

2/3 cup white sugar

1 tablespoon butter

Orange Fool Pudding

From the Oliver Wight Tavern

Combine ingredients in a heavy saucepan or double boiler. Cook very slowly until mixture thickens slightly. Do not boil, or it will curdle. Heat for about 25 minutes.

Chill in individual bowls or wine glasses. Serve very cold.

✦ YIELD ✦

Serves 6

Election Cake

From the Oliver Wight Tavern

If packaged yeast is used, mix water and sugar with yeast. Cream butter and sugar. Add eggs, beating after each addition.

Add yeast and blend well. Stir in 4 cups flour and beat for about 1 minute.

Combine currants or raisins with 3 cups remaining flour and add to rest of batter. Batter will be stiff, and flour may need to be worked in by hand. Add milk as required to make a soft, yet kneadable, dough.

Sprinkle remaining flour on a board. Knead for 10 minutes.

Divide dough in half. Use 5" × 9" loaf pans or two 8-inch pie plates. Let rise in greased pans in a warm place for 3–5 hours or overnight in the refrigerator.

Bake in preheated 350-degree oven for 50 minutes.

YIELD

Serves 12

1 cup yeast or 2 packages yeast
with 1 cup water and
1 tablespoon sugar

3/4 cup butter

1 cup sugar

2 eggs

8 cups flour, sifted

1/2 pound currants or raisins

1 cup milk

2 eggs

1 cup milk

1 1/2 cups flour or cornmeal

1 teaspoon baking powder

1/2 teaspoon cinnamon

1/8 teaspoon cloves

1/4 teaspoon salt

1 teaspoon nutmeg

5 tablespoons sugar

Fat to grease pan

Butter

Fritters

From the Oliver Wight Tavern

Beat the eggs and milk together with a whisk.

Sift flour or cornmeal with baking powder, cinnamon, cloves, salt, nutmeg, and 2 tablespoons of the sugar. Stir into the egg-and-milk mixture quickly.

Preheat skillet, griddle, or frying pan. When very hot, grease and drop 2–3 tablespoons batter for each fritter onto skillet. Turn when first side is browned. Grease griddle lightly after every two or three batches.

YIELD

Serves 4

OMNI PARKER HOUSE
Boston

Founded in 1855 by Harvey D. Parker, the Omni Parker House is the oldest of Boston's elegant inns and the longest continuously operating hotel in the United States. It is here that the brightest lights of America's golden age of literature—writers like Ralph Waldo Emerson, Henry David Thoreau, Nathanial Hawthorne, and Henry Wadsworth Longfellow—regularly met for conversation and conviviality in the legendary nineteenth-century Saturday Club. It is here that baseball greats like Babe Ruth and Ted Williams wined, dined, and unwound. And it is here that generations of local and national politicians—including Ulysses S. Grant, James Michael Curley, Franklin Delano Roosevelt, John F. Kennedy, and William Jefferson Clinton—have assembled for private meetings, press conferences, and power breakfasts.

Situated close to Boston's Theater District, the Omni Parker House has also played an important role for many of the nineteenth-century's finest actors. The Parker House has hosted such notables as Charlotte Cushman, Sarah Bernhardt, Edwin Booth, and the latter's handsome, matinee-idol brother, John Wilkes. During the past century, that list expanded to include stars of stage, screen, and television, including Joan Crawford, Judy Garland, Ann-Margret, and Marlow Thomas.

The site of the Omni Parker House is almost as old as Boston itself. When the Puritans first settled here, they built their first church, town house, freshwater spring, and stock and pillory within two blocks of where the Parker House stands today. The town was soon named Boston to honor the Lincolnshire town that many had just departed.

In 1825, Harvey D. Parker arrived in Boston Harbor on a ship from Maine. With less than $1 in his pocket, he was in need of employment. He first worked in a stable, moving up later to be a coachman for a wealthy Watertown woman. Whenever Parker brought the horse-drawn coach into Boston, he ate his noonday meal at a dark cellar cafe on Court Square, owned by John E. Hunt. In 1832, Parker bought Hunt's cafe for $432 and renamed it Parker's Restaurant. Excellent food and perfect service attracted a regular clientele. In 1854, with his sights set on grander horizons, Parker built an ornate, five-story, Italianate-style stone-and-brick hotel, faced in gleaming white marble. The first and second floors featured gracefully arched windows, while marble steps led from the sidewalk to the marble foyer within. Inside, thick carpets and fashionable horse-hair divans provided an air of sumptuous elegance. Above the front door, an engraved sign read simply, "Parker's."

The new hotel was an instant hit. Oliver Wendell Homes Sr. waxed eloquent about the food and friends he encountered at this most favorite of haunts. A reporter for the *Boston Transcript* fairly raved about the establishment in an October 1855 review. Visiting British author Charles Dickens marveled at the splendors of Boston's finest new hotel in a letter to his daughter: "This is an immense hotel, With all manner of white marble public Passages and public rooms. I live in a corner, high up, and have a hot and cold bath in the bedroom (connecting with the sitting room) and comforts not in existence when I was here before. The cost of living is enormous, but happily we can afford it."

Parker's experience with his first restaurant had taught him that catering to the gastronomic delights of Bostonians was as important as the beauty of his hotel. He hired the gourmet French chef Sanzian for an astonishing annual salary of $5000. The chef's fame drew large crowds and ongoing accolades. From a creative point of view, Parker's was not only the best but frequently the first as well. Boston cream pie (now the official dessert of the state of Massachusetts) and lemon meringue pie were perfected and popularized in nineteenth-century Parker House kitchens. The moist, fluffy, and internationally known Parker House roll was the inspired creation of an in-house German baker named Ward.

For many decades, Parker House rolls were packaged and shipped from the kitchens here to hotels, restaurants, and stores across the United States. Today, they are still served to Omni Parker House patrons—and imitated everywhere. The recipe for the rolls remained a well-kept secret until 1933, when Franklin and Eleanor Roosevelt requested that it be forwarded to them in Washington.

Harvey Parker and his successors ensured the excellence of the Parker's dining experience by hiring well-known European chefs. That tradition continued with talents such as longtime Parker's chef Joseph Ribas and a slew of rising restaurant stars, including Jasper White, Lydia Shire, and Emeril Lagasse. However, talent and fame were not restricted to the European and American chefs. Two notable revolutionaries spent time on the Parker House staff: Vietnamese leader Ho Chi Minh served as a baker in the bakeshop from 1911 to 1913, and Malcolm Little, also known as black activist Malcolm X, was a busboy in the early 1940s during the period of the Pearl Harbor invasion.

John Wilkes Booth, the least talented actor in that theatrical family, was a dedicated Confederate sympathizer. On April 5 and 6, 1865, John Wilkes was registered at the Parker House and was

seen eating in its restaurant. It was reported in the *Boston Evening Transcript* of April 15 that a man named "Borland . . . saw Booth at Edwards' shooting gallery [near Parker's], where Booth practiced pistol firing in various difficult ways such as between his legs, over his shoulder and under his arms." Eight days after leaving Boston, on April 14, 1865, John Wilkes Booth assassinated President Abraham Lincoln at Ford's Theatre in Washington, D.C.

Every U.S. chief of state, from Ulysses S. Grant through William J. Clinton, has passed through the hotel's portals, stayed in its suites, lobbied in its press room, imbibed in its bars, or dined in its restaurants. The rich century-and-a-half history of the Omni Parker House has established with visitors and natives alike an exceptional standard of excellence and innovation.

"A gourmet is just a glutton with brains."

—Philip W. Haberman

Omni Parker House
60 School Street
Boston, MA 02108
(617) 725-1630

6 eight-ounce filets of baby cod
(use only cod)

1 cup milk

1 teaspoon lemon juice

2 teaspoons Worcestershire sauce

Salt and pepper to taste

1/2 cup olive oil

2 teaspoons paprika

1/4 pound Ritz crackers,
finely crushed

1/2 pound butter, melted

1/2 cup white wine

Parker House Scrod

Marinate baby cod in milk, lemon juice, Worcestershire sauce, salt, pepper, olive oil, and paprika for 2 hours (the longer the better).

Remove from marinade and dip each fillet into cracker crumbs. Cover all surfaces well.

Preheat oven to 400 degrees.

Place fillets in buttered baking pan and drizzle with melted butter. Pour white wine into pan, being sure not to drizzle directly onto fish.

Bake until flaky, approximately 10 minutes. Do not overcook.

Place under broiler for a few minutes to finish and give color.

Tip: Serve with boiled or roasted new potatoes, a green vegetable, a wedge of lemon, and a dozen Parker House rolls.

YIELD

Serves 6

Parker House Rolls

About 3 1/2 hours before serving, combine in a large bowl 2 1/4 cups flour, sugar, salt, and yeast. Add 1/2 cup (1 stick) margarine or butter. With mixer at low speed, gradually pour 2 cups hot tap water (120–130 degrees) into dry ingredients.

Add egg and increase mixer speed to medium. Beat 2 minutes, scraping bowl with rubber spatula. Beat in 3/4 cup flour, or enough to make a thick batter. Continue beating for 2 minutes, occasionally scraping bowl. With spoon, stir in enough additional flour (about 2 1/2 cups) to make a soft dough.

Turn dough onto lightly floured surface and knead until smooth and elastic, about 10 minutes, working in more flour (about 1/2 cup) while kneading. Shape dough into a ball and place in large greased bowl, turning over so that top of dough is greased. Cover with towel and let rise in warm place (80–85 degrees) until doubled, about 1 1/2 hours. (Dough is doubled when two fingers pressed into dough leave a dent.)

Punch down dough by pushing down the center with a fist, then pushing the edges of the dough into center. Turn the dough onto a lightly floured surface. Knead lightly to make a smooth ball. Cover with a bowl for 15 minutes and let dough rest.

In 17.25" × 11.5" roasting pan, over low heat, melt re-

6 cups all-purpose flour

1/2 cup sugar

2 teaspoons salt

2 packages active dry yeast

1 cup (2 sticks) margarine or
   butter, softened

1 large egg

maining 1/2 cup margarine or butter. Tilt pan to grease bottom.

On a lightly floured surface with floured rolling pin, roll dough 1/2 inch thick. With floured 2 3/4-inch round cutter, cut dough into circles. Holding dough circle by the edge, dip both sides into melted margarine or butter in pan, then fold in half. Knead trimmings together, reroll, and cut more rolls. Cover pan with towel and let dough rise in warm place until doubled, about 40 minutes.

Bake rolls in a 400-degree oven for 15–18 minutes until browned.

YIELD

About 3 1/2 dozen

New England Clam Chowder

Wash clams, place in a pot with white wine and bouquet garni, and cook over medium heat.

In a skillet, sauté onions, celery, and carrots in butter until transparent. Add fish stock and clam juice. Cook 10 minutes. Add heavy cream, flour, chopped clams, potatoes, and chives. Cook another 15 minutes.

Check seasoning and serve. Garnish with bay leaf.

YIELD

Serves 8

---

12 chowder clams or cherrystone clams, chopped

8 ounces white wine

1 bouquet garni

1 onion, medium, finely chopped

1/2 cup celery, finely diced

1/2 cup carrots, diced

2 ounces butter

4 cups fish stock

2 cups clam juice

1 cup heavy cream

2 ounces flour

2 potatoes, large, finely diced

1 teaspoon chives, chopped

1 bay leaf

THE PUBLICK HOUSE
Sturbridge

Sturbridge stands astride two main New England arteries—the highways from Boston to New York and from Providence to Springfield. It was destined to be a main thoroughfare. The Indians used the "Old fordway to Tantiusque" when they traveled to Plymouth bringing corn to the Pilgrims. Later, the first white settlers traveled over the same route on their first westward journeys. Just thirteen years after the Pilgrims landed, John Oldham was traveling near the ford when Indians showed him strange pieces of "black rock." The first lead mine was discovered in America. The ford was the only place for travelers passing east and west to cross the river for many miles to the north and south. It also met the famous "Woodstock Path" running from Hartford and Providence to the north. Then, as now, the junction of routes made Sturbridge strategically important.

In 1754, when Benjamin Franklin was deputy postmaster of the thirteen colonies, he made a trip during which he visited most of the colonial post offices. This was not such a momentous undertaking as it sounds, for there were only twenty-eight then in existence. During the trip, the ever inventive Franklin affixed a mileage counter to the wheels of his carriage. Men accompanied him to set milestones along the roads to guide the mail carriers. According to local legend, the milestone in Sturbridge which reads "67 miles from Boston" was placed there as a result of this trip.

During the Revolutionary War, Sturbridge Common, which was given by the Saltonstalls "For Publick Use Forever," was the scene of great activity. Militia drilled on the green lawn. Stores were collected and hoarded. Col. Ebenezer Crafts himself personally equipped and supplied a company of cavalry for George Washington's army.

Again, in 1812, during the war with England, Sturbridge played a part in the prosecution of the struggle. No commerce could be carried on by sea between New York and Boston because of the embargo. As a result, goods were transported over land. A constant stream of four- and six-horse teams traveled between the two cities, and their route took them on the Boston Post Road through Sturbridge.

The Publick House on the common was a favorite stopping place for the teamsters. The inn's founder and keeper, Colonel Crafts, made frequent rounds and saw to it that each guest was satisfied and comfortable. In 1824 the tavern and the common were visited by General Marquis de Lafayette and his son, George Washington Lafayette. Over three thousand people assembled on the

green to greet the Revolutionary War hero. Great preparations were made at the Publick House for Lafayette. One good lady of the town carried her best china to the inn for the general's use. The general, however, was behind in his schedule, and the taproom's hospitality proved so great that he never made it any further into the inn.

Sturbridge itself came into being in 1730 when a drawing was made for homestead lots by such families as the Bournes, Plimptons, Hardings, Gelasons, Fiskes, and others. The name Sturbridge was adopted because an ancestor of one of the first settlers had come from Sturbridge in Worcester County, England. Actually, permission had been given by the general court for settlement and speculation a year earlier. Certain stipulations were made: Seven years from the date, fifty families had to be settled in houses that were at least eighteen feet square. The founders were also required to settle a "learned orthodox minister and lay out him a house lot equal to the other house lots."

Sturbridge became a cultural center, and in 1824 the present Sturbridge Fair was started for the purpose of awakening more interest in husbandry and the mechanical arts. By 1855, the fair was incorporated as a society, and the attendance each year increased rapidly. In 1834, the first balloon ascension in this part of New England was made from the fair grounds. The pilot was a Madame Carlotta of New York, and the records show that her performance increased the gate by $700 over the year before.

Colonel Crafts has left his equestrian profile on the Publick House sign, his name on the gracious bed and breakfast inn atop Fiske Hill, his legacy of majestic elms and maples shading the grounds, and his spirit of uncompromising good taste and hospitality on every greeting, eating, and meeting at the Publick House.

The Publick House
On the Common
Route 131, P.O. Box 187
Sturbridge, MA 01566-0187
(508) 347-3313
(800) PUBLICK (782-5425)

2 pints light cream

6 egg yolks

20 ounces lobster meat

1/8 pound butter

1/2 teaspoon paprika

1/3 cup sherry wine

Pinch of cayenne pepper

Salt to taste

TOPPING

2 cups fresh bread crumbs, grated

3/4 teaspoon paprika

3 tablespoons crushed potato chips

1 tablespoon Parmesan cheese

5 teaspoons butter, melted

4 tablespoons sherry

Publick House
Historic Inn & Country Lodge

Publick House Individual Lobster Pie

Heat light cream to a slow boil. Reduce heat and whisk in one egg yolk at a time.

In a separate pan, sauté lobster meat in butter and paprika. Add sherry and cook for 3 minutes. Add cayenne pepper, salt, and the cream sauce. Stir until the sauce bubbles and thickens.

Spoon the sauce into an 8" × 10" casserole dish or 6 individual casserole dishes, making sure to distribute the lobster meat evenly. Sprinkle with topping and brown in 450-degree oven.

TOPPING

Mix ingredients until well blended.

This may be prepared a day ahead and heated in a 350-degree oven for 1 hour.

YIELD

6 six-ounce portions

Publick House

Historic Inn & Country Lodge

Hermits

Combine sugar, kosher salt, vegetable shortening, cinnamon, milk powder, and baking soda in a stand-up mixer. Cream together for approximately 10 minutes, or until soft, pale, and translucent.

Slowly add the eggs in two stages.

Add the molasses and water and blend well.

Add the raisins and walnuts and stir slightly.

Sift the flour over the mixture and mix smooth.

Bake at 350 degrees in desired shape.

YIELD

4 dozen

1 pound brown sugar

1/2 ounce kosher salt

10 ounces vegetable shortening

1/8 ounce ground cinnamon

1/2 ounce milk powder

1/2 ounce baking soda

6 ounces eggs

8 ounces molasses

4 ounces water

1 pound raisins

8 ounces walnuts

2 pounds, 3 ounces cake flour, sifted

1 1/5 pound salt pork

1 pound Spanish onions, roughly chopped

1/2 head celery

1/3 pound margarine

1 1/5 pound Italian sausage

1 teaspoon poultry seasoning

2 pounds cornbread, crumbled

1/3 loaf of white sandwich bread, crumbled fine

8 ounces chicken stock

Kosher salt and ground white pepper to taste

Publick House

Historic Inn & Country Lodge

Cornbread and Sausage Stuffing

Purée the salt pork and reserve.

In a preheated stock pan, combine pork, onions, celery, margarine, sausage, and poultry seasoning and cook over medium heat for 15 minutes, or until slightly translucent.

Reduce the heat to low and add the cornbread and sandwich bread. Mix well.

Add the chicken stock and mix well again. Adjust the seasoning, if needed.

❧ YIELD ☙

Serves 16

THE RED LION INN
Stockbridge

Anna and Silas Bingham established a general store in Stockbridge on the road that connected Boston to Albany around 1773. It quickly evolved into a stagecoach stop, tavern, and inn under the sign of the red lion. Travel was hard and uncomfortable, and the Binghams' tavern rapidly became a popular and welcome rest stop for city travelers.

The Red Lion Inn also became popular with the locals. People could gather there, exchange pleasantries, and discuss the issues of the day. In late 1786, Daniel Shays led a group of local farmers and citizens in protest to British oppression and very high land taxes. Stockbridge was selected as the headquarters for what became known as "Shays' Rebellion." The Red Lion Inn's participation in these early events in the birth of the United States earned it a place in our history books.

In 1807, after Silas passed away, his widow sold the inn for $10,000 to Main Street store owner Silas Pepoon. Today, her role at the inn is commemorated by the popular Widow Bingham's Tavern. As time passed, the inn had a number of owners. In 1862, Charles H. Plumb and his wife, Mert (for whom the charming Plumb Room was named), began a ninety-year family-management dynasty. In 1893 the inn's operation would be taken over by Mr. Plumb's nephew Allen T. Treadway, aided by his assistant, James H. Punderson, whose daughter Molly became the third wife of famed illustrator Norman Rockwell.

The town of Stockbridge evolved over time. Early on, the area was mostly a farming community, with a few small factories in nearby towns. Guests of the inn and its tavern were hardy travelers of the stagecoach era, local farmers, and landowners. Soon, wealthy families had selected Stockbridge as a place to escape from city life. They built their "cottages" (which were really very grand homes) and settled in to enjoy the serenity of the countryside. The demands of expanding commerce and the arrival of the Housatonic Railroad in 1842 made the town easier to get to, and Stockbridge was no longer isolated from the outside world.

The literary colony established in nearby Lenox brought further changes to the area. Originally, the inn consisted of only eight rooms, with low ceilings, massive beams, and posts. In 1848, the Stockbridge House, as the Red Lion Inn was then known, expanded its facilities with an addition in order to accommodate the many new visitors. In 1884, the inn was enlarged once again to accommo-

date more than one hundred guests. As the inn grew, the quality of the amenities and food it offered improved, and the inn was able to satisfy the more sophisticated tastes of its stylish guests.

Mert Plumb was known for her appreciation of antique furniture, crockery, and pewter. She published a standing offer of "50 cents for a pitcher, $1 for an antique mirror" to add to the collection of the Plumb Hotel (as the inn was known then). Many of the antique furnishings seen in the Red Lion Inn today are from Mrs. Plumb's original collection.

In 1896, a fire almost destroyed the hotel, but Mrs. Plumb's collection of colonial china, pictures, apparel, and furniture was saved. Allen Treadway restored the inn, which opened again for business just eight months later. In 1904, Mr. Treadway was elected to Massachusetts's house of representatives and went on to serve in the state senate and then the U.S. Congress until 1944.

Until the inn was leveled by fire, its crest was a red lion with a green tail. The red lion was believed to be symbolic of the Crown, while the green tail indicated sympathy for the colonists during the Revolutionary War. At its rebirth in 1897 after the fire, Mr. Treadway unveiled a new crest in the form of a shield. At the top were a lion and two dates, 1773 and 1897, indicating the birth and rebirth of the inn. The body of the shield displayed a teapot, plate, Franklin stove, highboy, clock, and two large keys, representing the inn's collection of antiques. In the 1920s the shield was replaced with the lion we see today. It is plump and well fed, indicating the high quality of food served at the inn.

The inn was slated for destruction to make room for a gas station when it was rescued in 1968 by John and Jane Fitzpatrick. They had planned to use part of the main dining room and most of the kitchen for their growing Country Curtains business but became so taken with the inn and its history that they decided to continue its operation.

A large new kitchen and dining room were installed, and part of a former lounge became Widow Bingham's Tavern. All the public rooms were redecorated to better compliment the inn's wonderful collection of antique furniture, china, and pewter. On May 29, 1969, the Red Lion Inn opened for year-round business for the first time.

Beginning in 1974, several neighboring buildings were purchased and converted into guesthouses, including the former village firehouse, which is the most popular of all the accommodations in the inn. Following the tradition of Allen Treadway, Mr. Fitzpatrick served four terms as a Mas-

sachusetts state senator from 1972 to 1980. Once again, the Red Lion Inn became the center of political activity in the area. The inn is now owned and operated by the Fitzpatricks' daughter, Nancy.

The Red Lion Inn
30 Main Street
P.O. Box 954
Stockbridge, MA 01262-0954
(413) 298-5545

1/2 cup maple syrup

1 cup water

1/4 cup kosher salt

1/4 cup sugar

2 celery stalks, diced

1 carrot, diced

1/2 onion, diced

1 tablespoon juniper berries

2 bay leaves

4 pork tenderloins

Salt and pepper to taste

1 rosemary sprig

1 tablespoon extra virgin olive oil

Maple-Cured Pork Tenderloin

Mix maple syrup, water, kosher salt, sugar, celery, carrot, onion, juniper berries, and bay leaves.

Taste; liquid should be evenly salty and sweet, not too salty.

Add pork and marinate overnight.

Remove from liquid and season with salt, pepper, and chopped rosemary sprig.

Lightly brush with extra virgin olive oil.

Grill to medium.

Slice and serve with root vegetables.

YIELD

Serves 6–8

Red Lion Inn Cheddar Ale and Sausage Soup

Sauté onions, carrots, and celery in butter.

Add flour and cook 20 minutes on low.

Add ale and chicken stock, stirring until slightly thickened.

Add bratwurst, garlic, tomatoes, thyme, Old Bay, basil, oregano, cheddar cheese, and smoked cheddar and simmer 1 hour.

YIELD

Serves 16

1/2 onion, diced

1 carrot, diced

3 stalks celery, diced

1/2 cup butter

1/2 cup flour

1 1/2 pints ale

1 quart chicken stock

1 pound bratwurst, diced

2 tablespoon garlic, minced

1 cup canned tomatoes, diced

1 tablespoon dried thyme

1/2 tablespoon Old Bay seasoning

1 tablespoon dried basil

1 tablespoon dried oregano

1/4 pound cheddar cheese, shredded

1/4 pound smoked cheddar cheese, shredded

3 leeks, whites only, diced

3 cups carrots, diced

3 tablespoons butter

1 quart vegetable or chicken
    stock

1 tablespoon ground coriander

3 tablespoons cilantro, chopped

Salt and pepper to taste

1 cup heavy cream (optional)

Carrot and Coriander Soup

Sauté leeks and carrots in butter until slightly browned. Add stock and herbs. Simmer until tender, about 30 minutes. Purée and strain.

Garnish with chopped cilantro. Add salt and pepper to taste. To add richness, cream may be added to strained soup. Just return to slight boil.

Tip: On a hot day, serve chilled with a dollop of yogurt.

YIELD

Serves 4

UPSTAIRS ON THE SQUARE
Cambridge

~~~

One of the first fracases of the Revolutionary War occurred at the south corner of the stately building that overlooks Winthrop Park One. Built in 1906 by the Harvard fraternity the Pi Eta Club, a rival comedy and theatrical club to the Hasty Pudding Club, the building originally had its entrance facing the park and boasted a theater, a large stately staircase that led to a ballroom, and a kitchen.

After the Pi Eta Club moved to another building on lower Mount Auburn Street in the early 1970s, the building housed many different businesses over the next twenty years. When the entire block was redeveloped in the late 1990s, the building was bought by philanthropist Greg Carr, who turned it into the Market Theater. When he decided to build a new theater on Arrow Street, the building became home to two eateries, the pub Grendel's Den in the basement and, in 2002, UpStairs on the Square, a revival to the twenty-year-old UpStairs at the Pudding after its move from Holyoke Street.

UpStairs on the Square occupies the rest of the building, with two dining rooms and two kitchens, and has been widely acclaimed for its design and cuisine. Of particular note in the restaurant's design is its four working fireplaces, the "exuberant fenestration" of the second-floor round windows facing the park, and its lovely veranda room, also facing the park. The lavish designs are a throwback to 1940s glamour with a modern twist and reflect the highly personal style of owner and designer Deborah Hughes. The multifloored restaurant is filled with signature warmth, yet stimulating décor with a color scheme consisting of various hues of pink, corals, deep jewel tones, and accents of silver, gold, and copper leaf throughout. Wonderful leopard- and zebra-patterned carpets wrap the floors, and fanciful sconces and artwork adorn the walls.

In the first-floor Monday Club Bar, guests can enjoy sweeping views of the square while they sip and enjoy casual fare (such as the bar's signature pizzetta cooked to order in the pizza oven in the first-floor kitchen) in front of two working fireplaces. In the forefront of the high-ceilinged Monday Club Bar overlooking the park, the guests continue their tradition of dining en plein air with a sun-filled, sky-lit veranda room called the Zebra Room, full of light both in winter and summer and distinguished by a zebra carpet, as well as a wonderful view of the park and the life of the square beyond. The veranda can also be closed off by French doors to accommodate an intimate

 *118*

dinner party. On the mezzanine area overlooking the Monday Club Bar, a spectacular wine display housed in a glass-enclosed, custom-built, and temperature-controlled wine room exhibits over two thousand bottles. James Beard "Best Chef in the Northeast"–winner Susan Regis presides over the menu in the Monday Club Bar.

The UpStairs's Soirée Room reminds one of a colorful jewel box; the supper club is lit by fireplaces at each end of the room and distinguished by the famous and distinctive round windows facing the park. The signature pink linens and gracious, colorful surroundings complement the luxurious banquettes and the refurbished red and gold chairs from the restaurant's original location, making this main dining room an heir to the celebratory dining room at the Pudding. UpStairs on the Square celebrates the bounty of New England ingredients available with each new season and the handcrafted techniques that have made them popular over the years.

UpStairs on the Square
91 Winthrop Street
Cambridge, MA 02138
(617) 864-1933

Day Boat Lobster Salad with Orange Aioli and Fresh Harvest Beans

Add a good squeeze of fresh orange juice and the finely chopped orange zest to the mayonnaise and whisk.

Cut lobster pieces if necessary into large (3/4- to 1-inch pieces). Add salt, lemon juice, and lime juice.

Fold the lobster into the aioli and chill.

Add chives and garlic to canola oil. Pulse in Cuisinart or whisk rapidly. Salt to taste.

Blanch peas, corn, and beans quickly. Put in very cold water immediately to shock so that they retain their color.

PLATING
Place haricots verts crisscross around the perimeters of a dinner plate.

Place frisée in top center of the plate and cover with lobster salad.

Drizzle with chive oil (optional).

Strew a handful of fava and a small amount of corn kernels and peas randomly on the plate.

AIOLI
2 tablespoons fresh orange juice

1 teaspoon orange zest, finely chopped

1 cup good-quality commercial mayonnaise

Salt to taste

Juice of 1 lemon

Juice of 1 lime

2 pounds of fresh lobster meat (can be bought shelled and picked)

CHIVE OIL (OPTIONAL)
1 cup fresh chives, chopped finely

1 large clove garlic, chopped finely

1 cup canola oil

Salt to taste

SALAD
1 cup frozen baby peas, very quickly blanched (or fresh shelled peas)

1 cup frozen corn, very quickly blanched

1 cup frozen baby fava beans, very quickly blanched (or fresh baby favas)

2 cups haricots verts, with ends snipped

Segments of 2 oranges, trimmed
of all white membrane
(can be canned oranges or
mandarin orange segments)

1 head frisée lettuce

Arrange orange segments around perimeter of plate.

Decorate with flower petals.

Can be served with homemade or good-quality store-bought lemonade. Sugar the rims of each glass with pink-colored sugar. To create pink sugar, simply put a couple of drops of cherry juice (or red food coloring) into 1/2 cup granulated sugar on a plate and mix to get evenly colored sugar. Dunk the rim of each glass in a little lemonade, then circle the rim on the sugared plate to coat.

YIELD
Serves 6–8

Roasted Sweet Red Pepper Soup

Roast 20 extra large red peppers over an open flame. Do not let skins turn ashen and gray. After roasting, immediately blanch and peel blistered peppers. Roasted peppers are not enhanced by sitting in water. Drain and coarsely chop peppers.

Melt 1/4 pound of butter in one very large or two large heavy-bottomed sauté pans. Add balsamic vinegar, Anaheim peppers, Scotch bonnet peppers, and 2 rosemary sprigs. Simmer briefly, then add chopped red peppers. Cook for about 2 hours over very low heat. This process naturally caramelizes the peppers and melds the flavors together.

In a heavy-bottomed pot, reduce by half 1 quart of heavy cream. Remove from heat.

When peppers have softened considerably (about 2 hours), remove from heat. Cool slightly. Divide peppers into several batches and lightly purée in a blender, using the on/off switch. Do not overly homogenize.

Place in large enamel-coated cast iron soup pot and add cream. Cook slowly to combine flavors, approximately 20 minutes. Do not cover or allow to boil.

In a separate pot, combine onions, 1/4 pound of butter, 4 large rosemary sprigs, and garlic. Cook over

20 extra large red peppers

1/2 pound butter

1/2 cup balsamic vinegar

2 Anaheim peppers, coarsely chopped

2 Scotch bonnet peppers, coarsely chopped

6 sprigs rosemary

1 quart best-quality heavy cream

4 large white kitchen onions

1 head of garlic, chopped

Kosher salt to taste

low heat until wilted and softened, approximately 30 minutes. Purée when cooked and add to soup pot. Season to taste.

YIELD

Serves 6–8

Gazpacho with Rock Shrimp, Avocado, and Sweet Basil Pesto

This gazpacho can be made several days ahead of time and is served at room temperature rather than chilled like conventional gazpacho.

Seed 4 dozen plum tomatoes. Leave skin on and dice.

Remove stems from fresh basil.

Peel and very finely chop 6 or more cloves of garlic.

Mix garlic with basil in a blender. Add 1 tablespoon salt, 3/4 cup balsamic vinegar, and 1/2 cup good-quality extra virgin olive oil.

Combine the basil-garlic pesto and the plum tomatoes and leave at room temperature for several hours.

Quantities of vegetables can then be added. Your choice should depend on the quality of the ingredients and personal taste. All should be as finely diced as possible.

❧ YIELD ❧
Serves 12

---

4 dozen plum tomatoes, diced, skin on

6 bunches fresh basil

6 cloves garlic, chopped

1 tablespoon salt

3/4 cup balsamic vinegar

1/2 cup extra virgin olive oil

OTHER OPTIONS TO ADD JUST BEFORE SERVING

Whole yellow sweetheart Napa Valley tomatoes

Avocado, sliced

Grilled chicken

Grilled sweet corn, scraped off the cob

Grilled eggplant, sliced

Fresh little rock shrimp, marinated in lemon juice and good olive oil (especially recommended)

Dollop of basil walnut or other pesto

THE WAUWINET
Nantucket

A visit to Nantucket is like stepping into a time machine. From its narrow lanes to its cobblestone streets, history comes alive with its fantastic whaling heritage. Over eight hundred beautiful houses were built from 1740 to 1840, and most are still located in their original setting. This tiny island is home to one of the largest and most interesting historic districts in all of America. Two house museums are the 1723 Nathaniel Macy House and the 1844 Hadwen-Satler Mansion, both elegant monuments to the tremendous prosperity garnered through the whaling industry.

The Whaling Museum is home to exhibits that replicate the life onboard a whaling vessel and display the renowned scrimshaw collection with fine clarity. Guided walking tours of the Old Historic District give the visitor a true sense of the island. Amazing architectural designs are fine testaments to the proud people of Nantucket. Roof walks on many of the island's homes were used to spot incoming whale ships or for pouring a bucket of sand down a burning chimney.

The name Nantucket derives from an Indian word meaning "land far out to sea" or "faraway land." The island was populated by approximately fifteen hundred Native Americans of the Wampanoag tribe when it was discovered and charted by Capt. Bartholomew Gosnold in 1602.

The history of the settlement of Nantucket began in 1659 when Thomas Mayhew sold his interest to the nine original purchasers for £30 and two beaver hats, one for him and one for his wife. Only Boston and Salem were larger during the whaling days, making it at the time the third largest city in Massachusetts.

The Great Fire of 1846 destroyed the wharves and much of the business district. With the discovery of petroleum in the 1930s, the silting up of the harbor, and the California gold rush, the whaling industry experienced a marked decline. Soon an economic depression loomed and lasted until tourism became a major resource.

At the height of whaling, over eighty-eight ships sailed the world from Nantucket. The famous R. H. Macy department store in New York City was founded by a local. Maria Mitchell, the first woman astronomer and discoverer of a comet, was born and buried on the island.

Herman Melville based *Moby Dick* on the ramming of the ship *Essex* out of the harbor in 1820 by a very angry whale. The horse fountain near the Pacific Club on Main Street was donated to the community by William Hadwen Starbuck in 1885.

Wauwinet translated from the words of the Wampanoag tribe means "witness my hand." The Wauwinet House, whose original building was built in the mid-1800s, was a restaurant that served shore dinners to guests arriving by boat. In 1876 it became an inn and soon emerged as a Nantucket social center and a prime destination for northeasterners on summer vacation. In 1986, after the inn had fallen into quite some disrepair, it was purchased by Steve and Jill Karp, who restored it with great care and renamed it the Wauwinet, an Inn by the Sea.

The Wauwinet
120 Wauwinet Road
Nantucket, MA 02584
(508) 228-0145
(800) 426-8718

2 tablespoons canola oil

20 scallops

1/4 cup bacon, diced

1/2 cup butter

1 1/2 cups heavy cream

1/4 cup Parmesan cheese

1/2 teaspoon lemon juice

1 tablespoon chives, diced

Salt and pepper to taste

Nantucket Bay Scallops

In a large skillet, heat canola oil and sauté scallops on one side until golden brown.

Add bacon, butter, and heavy cream. Bring to a boil.

Add Parmesan cheese, lemon juice, chives, salt, and pepper.

PLATING

Place each scallop in an individual scallop shell, 5 per person.

YIELD

Serves 4

Skillet Roasted Black Sea Bass

Preheat oven to 375 degrees.

Split rib of leeks lengthwise and cut into diamonds.

Rinse in cold water, removing any sand. Sauté cut leeks until translucent.

Season both sides of fish with salt and pepper.

Heat canola oil on medium heat in skillet. Add fish, skin side down. Sauté for 5 minutes.

Place skillet in heated oven for 5 minutes.

Dredge Ipswich clams in buttermilk and then cornmeal.

Clams can either be pan fried or deep fried until crispy. Season to taste.

BOUILLABAISSE
Sauté tomato, fennel, white onion, and carrot until soft. Add tomato paste, white wine, threads of saffron, and clam juice.

Finish with 1 teaspoon of butter and strain.

PLATING
Place spoonful of leeks in center of plate. Place fish on top of leeks, skin side up. Place 2 clams on top of fish and pour bouillabaisse over dish.

YIELD
Serves 4

---

3 whole leeks

4 seven-ounce black sea bass fillets, skin on, pin bones removed

1/2 cup canola oil

8 Ipswich clams

1 cup buttermilk

1 cup cornmeal

Salt and pepper to taste

BOUILLABAISSE

1 tablespoon tomato, diced

1 tablespoon fennel, diced

1 tablespoon white onion, diced

1 tablespoon carrot, diced

1 teaspoon tomato paste

1/2 cup white wine

4 threads saffron

2 cups clam juice

1 teaspoon butter

2 teaspoons honey

1 teaspoon Dijon mustard

1 tablespoon Banyuls vinegar

1/4 cup olive oil

4 heirloom tomatoes, sliced

Sea salt and black pepper to taste

1 teaspoon Nuñez extra virgin
    olive oil

6 ounces Spanish feta cheese, cut
    into 4 pieces

1/4 teaspoon dried lemon zest

1/4 teaspoon pink peppercorns,
    crushed

1 teaspoon chives, sliced

4 leaves baby romaine lettuce

4 leaves baby red oak lettuce

4 leaves baby red leaf lettuce

4 leaves baby lola leaf lettuce

4 leaves Boston baby bibb lettuce

Fried shallot rings and basil oil,
    for garnish

Heirloom Tomato Salad

Preheat oven to 400 degrees.

Mix the honey, mustard, and vinegar together. Then, slowly whisk in the olive oil until it forms an emulsified vinaigrette.

Season the tomato slices with salt, pepper, and Nuñez olive oil.

Season the feta cheese with the dried lemon zest, pink peppercorn, and chives. Bake the cheese for 2 minutes.

Dress the romaine, red oak, red leaf, lola leaf, and Boston baby bibb lettuces with the vinaigrette and season with salt and pepper.

Place the tomatoes on the plate. Top with the feta cheese and then the lettuces.

Garnish with fried shallots and basil oil.

YIELD

Serves 4

XV BEACON HOTEL
Boston

XV Beacon occupies the site of the Bromfield Mansion, built in 1722 by wealthy Boston merchant Edward Bromfield. Plans for the commercial building at XV Beacon Street were drawn in 1903 by renowned Boston architect William Gibbons Preston, and the building was completed in 1905. The Classical Revival–style building's first occupant was the Boston Transit Commission, credited as the nation's first public transportation agency, which built the nation's first subway system.

The XV Beacon building was deeded to the city of Boston in 1920, and the Boston School Committee occupied the building until 1976, managing the busing crisis from its offices there during the 1960s and 1970s. Between 1976 and 1997, the Department of Public Facilities and its successor, the Department of Neighborhood Development, were housed in the high-rise.

In 1997 the property was transferred to the Boston Redevelopment Authority. It was later purchased by Paul Roiff, a prominent Boston developer and entrepreneur, who converted it into XV Beacon, an elegant sixty-room boutique hotel. XV Beacon is handsomely modernist, yet retains accents of "Old Boston," such as the building's original cage elevator and its cast-brass lit railing with brass newel post in the lobby. The grand marble staircase adds to the Beaux-Arts grandeur.

Artwork is prominent throughout XV Beacon; its collection includes works by artists like Gilbert Stuart, Martha Lloyd, Joe Greene, Tony Evanko, and Ben Freeman, who were specially commissioned to create pieces for the hotel. XV Beacon is also home to Mooo, one of the newest steak house experiences in Boston. Guests enjoy easy proximity to one of the city's most prominent and historic neighborhoods, Beacon Hill. The hotel is located just a block from Boston Common and the gold-domed Massachusetts State House.

XV Beacon is a modernist hotel in a turn-of-the-century, ten-story Beaux Arts building. The façade's first two stories are cast iron, ornamented with gilded shields. The third story is a limestone band supporting five stories of roman brick. The ninth and tenth floors are limestone-fluted columns with mosaic inserts, capped by an opulent, oversized copper cornice.

The hotel's upper floors have no more than seven guest rooms apiece. Every room is individually designed so that no two rooms are alike. Each floor contains either a two-room suite or adjoining rooms that can be converted into a two-room suite. Each room has its own color scheme and furniture design, drawn from palettes of taupe, cream, and espresso. All rooms have fireplaces and

built-in mahogany wall units that contain in-room entertainment systems and private bars. Every custom fireplace features a stainless steel chimney breast and a floating chimney piece.

Mahogany walls surround the lobby, and a cozy fireplace offers a warm welcome. Located on the lobby level are the lounge, the bar, and the dining room. Formerly known as the Federalist, Mooo is an upscale steak house with a unique wine collection.

Tucked away beneath Mooo is the Wine Cellar, one of Boston's most unusual private dining rooms. Appointed with rich mahogany tables, the cellar seats up to forty-five dining guests or accommodates up to seventy-five people for a reception. This exclusive room showcases one of the most extensive wine collections in the country.

The granite foundation of the Wine Cellar is that of the Edward Bromfield Mansion, built in 1722. With its double-vaulted ceiling, the caged-glass walls hold wines ranging from today's notables to the most obscure "cult wines." A Roman mosaic depicts two deer amid flowers, amphorae, and fish heads dating from the fourth or fifth century AD.

In 2007, the elegant building that houses XV Beacon Hotel was listed on the National Register of Historic Places, a federal designation that bestows honor on one of Boston's architecturally and historically significant buildings.

"Fish, to taste right, must swim three times—in water, in butter, and in wine."

—Polish proverb

XV Beacon Hotel
15 Beacon Street
Boston, MA 02108
(888) 229-0684

Wellfleet Oyster Stew

Open oysters carefully, being careful not to puncture the delicate meat inside the shell.

Save all the liquid from inside the oyster shell and set aside with the meat.

In a saucepan, heat up a bit of olive oil on medium-low heat and add the leeks and bacon. Sauté, stirring frequently, until the leeks are soft and the bacon is a bit crispy.

Add the sherry and allow it to simmer for 4 or 5 minutes until it reduces by 2/3.

Add the heavy cream and bring to a simmer. Add oysters and oyster liquid, bring to a simmer, and season with salt, pepper, and thyme. Ladle into four soup crocks, top with a little spoon of butter and toasted bread, and sprinkle with a little smoked paprika. Serve immediately.

YIELD

Serves 4

36 Wellfleet oysters scrubbed well with cold water

2 tablespoons olive oil

1 large leek, washed and diced small

6 ounces applewood-smoked bacon, diced small

12 ounces aged sherry wine

1/2 pint heavy cream

Kosher salt

Cracked black pepper

2 tablespoons fresh thyme leaves

4 teaspoons unsalted Vermont butter

4 ounces cubed white bread, tossed in olive oil and toasted in oven at 300 degrees until golden brown

1 tablespoon smoked paprika

1/2 gallon water

3 tablespoons white vinegar

2 tablespoons dill, chopped

1/2 cup hollandaise sauce

1/2 cup Maine crab

2 tablespoons butter

8 large eggs

4 slices smoked salmon

8 English muffins, toasted

HOME FRIES

2 large Idaho potatoes, diced and
　　blanched in 3 tablespoons
　　clarified butter

1/2 Spanish onion, diced

1/2 red bell pepper, diced

1/2 yellow bell pepper, diced

1 tablespoon smoked paprika

1 tablespoon garlic powder

1/2 cup scallions, chopped

Salt and freshly ground pepper
　　to taste

Poached Eggs with Smoked Salmon, Crab, and Dill Hollandaise

In a shallow saucepan, bring 1/2 gallon of water to a simmer. Add 3 tablespoons of white vinegar (helps eggs stay together).

Mix the dill and hollandaise sauce.

Warm the crab gently in butter.

Poach the eggs in the simmering water.

Cut each slice of smoked salmon in half.

HOME FRIES

Sauté potatoes in clarified butter until they start to brown.

Add onions and peppers and continue to sauté until soft and crispy.

Add paprika and garlic powder.

Finish with scallions and season to taste with salt and pepper.

PLATING

Place the smoked salmon on the toasted English muffins. Spoon about 1 tablespoon of crab onto the smoked salmon. When the eggs are ready, lay the poached eggs on top of the crab, sauce the eggs with the dill hollandaise, and serve.

❧ YIELD ❧

Serves 4

8 lobster bodies, gills removed

2 large onions, diced medium

2 cloves garlic, crushed

1 large carrot, peeled and diced

2 stalks celery, diced medium

1/4 cup tomato paste

1 bay leaf

1 teaspoon black peppercorns

1 cup quality brandy

1 cup dry aged sherry

3 quarts heavy cream

1/4 bunch chervil

Lobster Bisque

Preheat oven to 350 degrees.

Roast lobster bodies until bright red and fragrant. Remove meat and reserve.

In a large pot, sauté onion, garlic, carrot, and celery until lightly caramelized.

Add tomato paste, bay leaf, and black peppercorns.

Cook slowly over low heat until tomato paste becomes slightly darker red and roasted.

Add lobster meat and stir through, crushing lobster as desired.

Add brandy and sherry over low heat, then turn to medium and reduce by half (be careful as alcohol may flame until cooked off).

Add cream, stir through, and simmer until reduced to desired consistency and thickness.

PLATING

Garnish with cooked claw meat removed from shell and sprig of chervil.

YIELD

Serves 8

Vermont

BASIN HARBOR CLUB
Vergennes

When Samuel de Champlain followed a band of Algonquin Native Americans into what is now Lake Champlain, he discovered an area uninhabited except by the Iroquois and Algonquin Indians. They had found the broad valley to be one of their favorite hunting and fishing places. Arrowheads, stone axes, and other Native American artifacts provide clear evidence of their habitation and can still be found on the banks of many streams flowing into the lake.

Around 1700, the French made many attempts to establish colonies in this area. Despite enthusiastic support from the king of France, the efforts were largely a failure. One colony apparently thrived for a time at Basin Harbor, but archives fail to reveal any detailed records of this early settlement. There is an ancient cemetery at the start of the North Harbor nature walk with a number of graves, and when archeologists opened one, they found a sword with an inscription indicating that the owner was a French officer. Among those early settlers, there was at least one unknown Frenchman who gave his name to the harbor. A map bearing the date 1730 shows the name "Bason Harbour."

When the French and Indian Wars ended, many settlers returned to the Champlain Valley. The township of Ferrisburgh, where Basin Harbor is located, was chartered in 1762 in a document issued by Benning Wentworth, the colonial governor of New Hampshire. Rapid settlement of the area was hindered for some time as there was a dispute over ownership of the area. Both New York and New Hampshire claimed the territory. Also, the lake was a well-traveled warpath for a period extending well beyond the Revolutionary War.

After the war for independence, former soldiers were granted large plots of land as partial pay. In this manner, David Callander, Ira Brydia, and others secured title to the land surrounding Basin Harbor. In the first deed of record, date 1790, David Callander sold ten acres on the north point of Basin Harbor to one Platt Rogers for £50, which at that time was about $25 an acre. In June of the following year, Rogers purchased a much larger plot from Ira Brydia and started to build the first permanent residence at Basin Harbor, the site of the present-day Homestead.

Rogers set up a shipyard at Basin Harbor, which eventually provided several of the boats used by the federal government during the War of 1812 for its navy on Lake Champlain. An early sail ferry to New York was also constructed here. When Rogers died, the property was divided up, and

his daughter and her husband, James Winans, continued to operate the inn or tavern on the site of the present-day Homestead.

When the War of 1812 ended, regular steamboat service on Lake Champlain brought about changes at Basin Harbor. The Champlain Canal opened to connect Lake Champlain with the Hudson River. This created new opportunities for trade on the lake. While the Homestead, as the oldest continuously operating inn on Lake Champlain, had a long record of serving travelers, the lodge on the south shore was relatively new to the inn-keeping field.

In 1882, Ardelia Beach acquired the Basin Harbor farm consisting of 225 acres with a farmhouse and outbuildings. Within four years, the place had been remodeled so that a few guests could be entertained. In 1909, her nephew, Allen P. Beach, then a sophomore at the University of Vermont, came to work with her to assist in the operation of the lodge. When Ardelia died that same year, Allen Penfield Beach, or A. P., became the inspirational force behind Basin Harbor's development.

Eventually, the farming aspects of the business were phased out. In 1927 the first nine holes of golf were built on what had been farmland. The first electrical line came down the road from Vergennes in 1929. The Homestead property was acquired in the 1930s, and cottages began to spring up on the north side of the harbor. The Basin Harbor Club now consisted of the Homestead as well as the lodge and a large number of cottages.

When A. P. died in 1963, his descendents took up the tradition of operating the resort. The Beach family remains committed to providing a retreat from daily cares, where body and soul can rejuvenate.

Basin Harbor Club
4800 Basin Harbor Road
Vergennes, VT 05491
(802) 475-2311
(800) 622-4000

MUSHROOM MIXTURE

1/4 cup sun-dried tomatoes

1/2 cup boiling water

1/4 cup butter

1 tablespoon garlic, chopped

1/2 teaspoon crushed red pepper

1/4 tablespoon dried thyme or
    1/2 teaspoon fresh

1/2 pound button mushrooms,
    sliced

1/2 pound portobello mushrooms,
    sliced

1/4 cup white wine

1/2 tablespoon lemon juice

2 1/2 cups artichoke quarters

1/8 cup fresh basil, chopped

1/2 tablespoon fresh parsley,
    chopped

Salt and pepper to taste

CROSTINI

Whole clove fresh garlic

Grated Asiago cheese

Olive oil

French bread, sliced

Mushroom Sauté with Herb Cheese Crostini

MUSHROOM MIXTURE

Place sun-dried tomatoes in a bowl and soak with boiling water. Drain tomatoes and slice thinly. Set aside. Melt butter in skillet and add garlic, red pepper, and thyme. Sauté 1 minute. Then add button and portobello mushrooms. Sauté until brown, about 10 minutes. Add wine, lemon juice, artichokes, sun-dried tomatoes, and spices and simmer for 2 minutes. Chill.

CROSTINI

Place whole peeled garlic and Asiago cheese in blender and mix. Drizzle in olive oil while blending until mix reaches a consistency for spreading on thin slices of French bread. Toast until light brown.

PLATING

Warm mushroom mixture. Place herbed cream cheese or goat cheese in small ramekin and serve with toasted crostini and mushrooms.

YIELD

4 cups

Chicken Salad Veronique

Mix together all ingredients and chill before serving.

❧ YIELD ❧

Serves 4–6

3 cups (1 pound) cooked chicken

1 1/2 cups seedless red grapes, halved

1/2 cup walnuts, chopped

1/2 cup watercress, stems removed, chopped

2 scallions, chopped

1/4 cup mango chutney (optional)

1 cup mayonnaise

Salt and pepper to taste

Maple Brioche Bread Pudding

6 eggs

4 or more egg yolks

3 1/2 cups half-and-half

1 cup sugar (white)

1/2 cup maple syrup

3 cups brioche, cubed and toasted

In a separate bowl, beat together eggs and yolks. In a pan, blend half-and-half, sugar, and maple syrup and bring to a boil. Slowly whisk hot mixture into the eggs and yolks.

Divide the brioche cubes into 6 six-ounce ramekins or custard cups. Pour the custard mixture over the cubes. Bake for approximately 25–35 minutes at 325 degrees in a water bath until set. Putting the ramekins in a roasting pan with water will work well.

YIELD

Serves 6

THE EQUINOX
Manchester Village

⊱————————————————⊰

When the French threat to Britain's North American colonies ended in 1763, the British government decided that the colonies themselves should pay taxes to support the cost of keeping them in the empire. As the British parliament imposed both new taxes and laws, the colonists began to rebel. Since they had no representation in the governing body, they felt that it was completely unfair that they be compelled to pay taxes they did not agree with.

In Manchester Village, the Council of Safety held a meeting in 1769 at the Marsh Tavern. Ethan Allen's younger brother, Ira Allen, proposed that the colonists confiscate the property of all British loyalists to raise money to equip a regiment of the "Green Mountain Boys" for the coming American Revolution. About the time that the council approved this idea, the owner of the tavern, William Marsh, had decided that the British would win the war, and he gave his allegiance to them. When the Marsh Tavern itself became the first property to be expropriated, Marsh fled to Canada.

Thaddeus Munson purchased the Marsh Tavern in 1780 and operated it until he built a new inn next door. Munson's inn then changed ownership three times, with Martin Vanderlip adding the fluted columns to the front in 1839, which would eventually become a trademark of the hotel. The columns still stand today . . . 285 feet across.

In 1853, the two-hundred-room Equinox House was established. The original Orvis homestead was incorporated as the north wing. Its homestead fireplace, inscribed "L.C. Orvis 1832," still provides guests with a warm and inviting fire on a cold evening. The north wing is now the "working" part of the hotel. It encompasses several guest rooms, as well as the colonnade, lobby areas, front desk, gift shop, administrative offices, and the present Marsh Tavern, Chop House, and Falcon Bar.

The hotel is named for Mount Equinox, which stands directly behind it. In the early 1900s, the symbol of the hotel was an Indian above the word "Equinox," giving rise to the belief that the Indians gave the hotel its name. However, there were never any Equinox Indians. The name Equinox comes from the fact that the Vermont surveyor general, Colonel Partridge, reached the summit of the mountain on the autumnal equinox in 1823.

Rising over thirty-eight hundred feet above the village of Manchester, Mount Equinox is the tallest peak in the Taconic Range. A tourist attraction in its own right, the mountain is one of the most beautiful in the state during the fall foliage season. The scenic drive to its top yields a vast panorama of southern Vermont beauty.

Manchester Village is filled with American history. The hotel itself is on Manchester's village green. The statue there, erected in 1891, is not of Ethan Allen, as many would guess, but instead represents the colonial soldier who fought for the colony's independence. Also found on the village green are the two-hundred-year-old congregational church, the Bennington County Court House, another vintage structure with white columns (a small reflection of the grand old hotel), and an old music hall.

The Equinox has been host to many illustrious guests. Presidents William Howard Taft, Ulysses S. Grant, Theodore Roosevelt (who gave a campaign speech on the front lawn), and Benjamin Harrison, as well as Vice President James S. Sherman, all visited in their time. Mary Todd Lincoln visited the Equinox with her two sons during the summer of 1864 while the president pursued the war. She enjoyed her visit so much that she made reservations to return again the following year with the president. A special suite was constructed in anticipation of the president's visit, but he was assassinated April 14, 1865. Their son, Robert Todd Lincoln, also loved the area so much that he built his summer estate, Hildene, just down the road.

Among the hotel's unique offerings was its supply of pure spring water from Mount Equinox, advertised in the 1880s as "the best and purest water . . . a great luxury to the guests." It became so popular that the Equinox Springs Company began bottling and selling the water. It remained in business until 1920.

The local industry in nineteenth-century Manchester was marble, and the streets were literally paved with it. There are over four miles of marble sidewalks. The first of these was constructed in front of the hotel in 1832. Because they proved extremely slippery when wet, the marble in front of the hotel was replaced with textured pavers, but the original marble still serves as a border.

Although shuttered in 1972, the Equinox was completely renovated and reopened in July 1985 as a resort hotel and conference center, reviving the rich tradition it had provided to southern Vermont for 239 years. Offering six different architectural styles and seventeen different structures,

the Equinox has been known in various times as the Marsh Tavern, Thaddeus Munson's New Inn, Widow Black's Inn, Vanderlip's Hotel, the Taconic, the Orvis Hotel, and the Equinox House. It stands today as a symbol of the history and lifestyle of New England over the past two centuries.

The Equinox
3567 Main Street, Route 7A
Manchester Village, VT 05254
(800) 362-4747

2 one-and-a-half-pound Maine
lobsters, meat removed

8 pieces asparagus

2 tablespoons lemon oil

4 bundles each chervil and mâche

MUSTARD VINAIGRETTE

3 tablespoons white wine vinegar

2 tablespoons Dijon mustard

3/4 cup canola oil

Salt and white pepper

Chilled Lobster and Asparagus Salad

Slice lobster tails into 1/2-inch medallions. Arrange on plate in a circle. Trim asparagus of tough ends about half way up the stalk. Mist with lemon oil, place on a grill, and cook for about 2 minutes. Remove and slice in half lengthwise. Then cut into 1-inch pieces. Set aside.

Toss the mâche and chervil together with the lemon oil and place in a bundle on top of the lobster meat. Tuck the claw meat just under the greens. Place the asparagus in the greens at different angles. Drizzle the mustard vinaigrette around the plate.

MUSTARD VINAIGRETTE

Combine the vinegar and mustard in a medium mixing bowl. Whisk to incorporate. Slowly add the canola oil into the mustard and let it emulsify. Finish with salt and white pepper. If dressing becomes too thick, adjust with a small amount of water.

YIELD
Serves 4

Roasted Butternut Squash Soup

Cut the butternut squash lengthwise and place cut side down on a cookie sheet that has been sprayed lightly with nonstick cooking oil. Roast squash in a 350-degree oven for about 50 minutes until squash is soft and caramelized. Remove meat with a spoon.

Heat oil in a large, heavy-bottomed saucepan over medium heat. Add the onions and garlic. Sauté until soft and the onions are slightly brown.

Add the squash to the pan with the onions and garlic. Let this cook for about 10 minutes.

Add chicken or vegetable broth and let simmer for about 40 minutes, stirring occasionally. Remove from heat and purée carefully in a blender. Soup should be a smooth consistency. Return to the saucepan and adjust seasoning and consistency.

To adjust the seasoning, add salt and pepper to taste. Then add balsamic vinegar.

PLATING

Ladle the soup into four bowls and top with apples.

YIELD

1/4 gallon

3 butternut squash

1 tablespoon canola oil

1/2 medium onion, yellow, sliced

1 clove garlic, chopped

1/2 gallon chicken or vegetable broth

Salt and cracked black pepper to taste

1 tablespoon balsamic vinegar

1/2 Granny Smith apple, julienned

GREEN MOUNTAIN INN

Stowe

Although Stowe was chartered as a town in 1763, the first settlers did not arrive until thirty years later in 1793. By 1800, the population had grown to 316, and most of the land had been sold and settled. Agriculture and lumber were essential industries for Stowe in the early years. At one point, over 75 percent of the land in Stowe and most of Vermont was open land that had been cleared for lumbering and agriculture. As many as eight thousand sheep grazed the hills and valleys of Stowe in those days.

Stowe's farming fortunes fluctuated with the rest of New England agriculture as most of Vermont shifted from sheep to dairy farms with more than one hundred farms located in Stowe. Nine of these operating farms remain today. This change has allowed most of the land to reforest, with only 25 percent remaining as cleared land.

The Green Mountain Inn was built by Peter C. Lovejoy as a private dwelling in 1833. In 1850, Peter traded the residence with Stillman Churchill for a 350-acre farm. Churchill added two brick wings and a dance hall to the original building, built a double porch in front, and named it the Mansfield House. Because of financial difficulties, he had to borrow money from W. H. H. Bingham and later lost the property when Bingham foreclosed on the mortgage.

By the mid-1800s, Stowe had developed into a popular summer resort due to its good transportation connections and spectacular mountain scenery. The toll road to the top of Mount Mansfield was completed by 1870. Summit House on the top of Mount Mansfield was finished just as the Civil War broke out.

Known as the "Big Hotel," the Mansfield House burned in 1889. A large stable housing over one hundred horses, tack, carriages, and stable hands was located behind the Big Hotel at the present site of the Green Mountain Inn's annex wing. This barn was eventually torn down as a fire hazard in 1953, and several of the original beams were used in constructing the Whip Bar.

The Mansfield House continued to be operated as a hotel and eventually was transferred to W. P. Bailey, who operated the property for several years as the Brick Hotel. In 1893, Mark C. Lovejoy purchased the Brick Hotel and renamed it the Green Mountain Inn.

The Depot Building, located next to the Green Mountain Inn, was built in 1897 to support the Mount Mansfield Electric Railway. Running just eleven miles between Waterbury and Stowe, this train carried both passengers and freight until 1932. The Depot Building is now connected to the inn by a bridge, housing sixteen guest rooms and a variety of shops.

Summer tourism remained an important part of Stowe's economic life until World War I. A new era was then born in Stowe when three resident Swedish families took to traveling around town on long, narrow, wooden boards with upturned ends. The citizens were curious about this new means of transportation, and several townspeople became hooked on this strange new sport. Skiing found a home in Stowe, and this turning point was perhaps the beginning of Stowe's real destiny.

Stowe held its first winter carnival in 1921 with ski jumping, skating, and a variety of winter events. However, downhill skiing never really developed in Stowe until after the Great Depression, when the Civilian Conservation Corps began clearing ski trails on Mount Mansfield. The first one built was the Bruce Trail that leads from the present site of the Octagon to Ranch Camp. The Bruce Trail is now incorporated into the Mount Mansfield Ski Touring trail system.

More trails and ski schools caused the town of Stowe to expand steadily over the years. Stowe soon established its reputation as one of the premier ski resorts in the world.

In 1982, the Inn of Stowe was purchased by Marvin Gameroff, a Canadian visitor to Stowe who fell in love with the property. It was transferred to the Gameroff Trust, the present owner, and a massive restoration project was completed to honor the 150th birthday of the building. Modern safety features were added during the restoration, including a full sprinkler/fire alarm system, internal fire stairs, exits, and new wiring. A swimming pool, the Whip Bar & Grill, cable television, air-conditioning, meeting space, and a fully equipped health club with fireside lounge area were also added to the facilities.

The year 2000 brought the last phase of the inn's overall expansion, the Mansfield House. This 28,000-square-foot addition features twenty-two beautiful guest rooms and a beautifully appointed common living room. Two- and three-bedroom town homes were added for those looking for full kitchens, living rooms, and other amenities. The main building and adjacent Depot Building are listed as numbers 13 and 14 on the National Register of Historic Places.

Over the years, the inn has hosted many famous visitors, including Lowell Thomas, who made regular broadcasts from the inn; President Gerald Ford, who stayed here as a student on a modeling assignment for *Look* magazine; and President Chester A. Arthur, who acted in a theatrical production at the inn.

Today, Stowe is the largest town in land area in the state with over fifty thousand acres. Vermont's highest peak, Mount Mansfield, and some of the finest agricultural land and forest in the state are located within this area.

"There is no love sincerer than the love of food."

—George Bernard Shaw

The Green Mountain Inn
18 Main Street
Stowe, VT 05672
(800) 253-7302
(802) 253-7301

New England Clam Chowder

Sauté the bacon, onions, and celery slowly. Then add the parsley, creamed and whole corn, cream, milk, Tabasco, stock, salt, and pepper. Simmer for 45 minutes. Add potatoes and thicken with the roux.

❧ YIELD ❧
Serves 12

4 strips bacon, chopped

1 onion, chopped

1 cup celery, chopped

1/4 cup fresh parsley

28 ounces creamed corn

28 ounces whole corn

1/2 quart heavy cream

2 quarts milk

6 drops Tabasco

8 cups turkey or chicken stock

Salt and pepper to taste

4 cups potatoes, cooked and diced

Roux, 50 percent butter and 50 percent flour

1/8 cup yeast

1/2 cup hot water,
    105–110 degrees

1 1/2 cups quick oats

3 cups water

1/3 cup butter, melted

1 3/4 tablespoons salt

3/4 cup honey

7 1/2 cups flour

Honey Oatmeal Bread

In a bowl mix yeast and hot water and let stand. Next, mix oats, water, butter, salt, and honey in a large mixing bowl. Add yeast and hot-water mixture. Mix together. Add flour. Set to rise. Divide dough and knead. Shape into three loaves and put into greased standard loaf pans. Let rise. Bake at 325 degrees for 35 minutes.

Optional: Coat top of loaves with egg-white mixture and oats before baking.

YIELD

3 loaves

Vermont Maple-Pumpkin Cheesecake

CRUST

Combine graham cracker crumbs, ginger, and cinnamon. Stir in melted butter. Press onto the bottom of a 9-inch spring form pan. Bake for 10 minutes at 325 degrees.

FILLING

Beat cream cheese until smooth, add sugar, and blend well. Blend one egg at a time. Add the pumpkin, maple syrup, cinnamon, nutmeg, and ginger.

Stir until smooth. Spoon filling into crust-lined pan. Bake at 325 degrees for 45 minutes, or until center appears set when gently shaken.

TOPPING

Combine sour cream, sugar, and maple syrup. Spread evenly over baked cheesecake and bake for 5 more minutes. Cool for 15 minutes, then loosen crust from pan. When cool, cover and chill at least 4 hours.

YIELD

Serves 8

CRUST

1 cup graham cracker crumbs

1/2 teaspoon ground ginger

1/2 teaspoon ground cinnamon

3 tablespoons butter, melted

FILLING

3 ounce package cream cheese, softened

3/4 cup sugar

6 eggs

1 1/2 cup canned pumpkin

1 tablespoon maple syrup

1/2 teaspoon cinnamon

1/2 teaspoon nutmeg

1/2 teaspoon ginger

TOPPING

1 cup sour cream

1/4 cup sugar

1 teaspoon maple syrup

THE INN AT SAWMILL FARM
West Dover

Originally known as the Winston Farm, the Inn at Sawmill Farm was built on the site of the first business in West Dover, Vermont, a sawmill. Consisting of over twenty acres in West Dover, the farm is a stone's throw from Mount Snow. It was purchased by the Williams family in 1967 and was originally intended to be their personal ski retreat. They decided almost immediately to leave their home and business in Atlantic City and go into the inn business in Mount Snow, Vermont.

As Rod and Ione Williams have explained many times to their guests, "Who were we to invade a field so foreign to our professions of architecture and interior design? Many of our guidelines were our own responses to the many inns we had previously visited. We have tried to capture and mold what we most enjoyed from each of them."

The Inn at Sawmill Farm opened with just nine guest rooms, a living room, a kitchen, and one dining room. Ione ran the kitchen and did the books, and Rod took care of the dining room and guests. The family lived in the original farmhouse, which has since been converted into four additional guest rooms. Two years later, upon his graduation from college, their son, Brill, joined them and eventually took over the kitchen. He is now the chef/owner.

The years have seen the addition of more dining and office space. An eighteenth-century barn with hand-hewn beams and weathered siding became three dining rooms with a cozy copper-topped bar, a large lounge with soaring ceilings and a fireplace, and a library game room where the hayloft used to be. Additional rooms were also created. There are two ponds for trout fishing, an outdoor pool, two gazebos, and a tennis court.

All twenty-one rooms are different, reflecting Ione's decorating talents. The ten in the main house are spacious, decorated in rich fabrics and antiques. A few have decks for sitting out in the summer. Eleven fireplace rooms, some with Jacuzzis and canopy beds, are in nearby buildings: three in the Ciderhouse, four in the Farmhouse, and one each in the Spring House, Wood Shed, and Mill House.

Recently opened is the new Carriage House, which once served as a barn in the eighteenth century. Completely restored and renovated, it is now a one-bedroom suite appointed with antiques, fabrics, and custom upholstered furniture of the federal period. Utterly private, its tall arched windows and a wrap-around deck overlook a two-acre trout pond and gardens.

Built in 1902, Blantyre is a luxury hotel situated in the Berkshires. Photo by Sean McLaughlin, courtesy of Blantyre.

Chatham Bars Inn has been a renowned Cape Cod landmark since its opening in 1914. Photo courtesy of Chatham Bars Inn.

Emerson Inn by the Sea is located in Rockport, Massachusetts, along the coast of scenic Cape Ann. Photo courtesy of Emerson Inn by the Sea.

Jurys Boston Hotel is ideally located in the heart of Boston's Back Bay area. Photo courtesy of Jurys Boston Hotel.

The Berkshire's Red Lion Inn is one of the few New England inns that has operated continuously since the eighteenth century. Photo © Kristian Septimius Krough, courtesy of the Red Lion Inn.

UpStairs on the Square is centrally located in Cambridge's Harvard Square. Photo courtesy of UpStairs on the Square.

Vermont's Basin Harbor Club overlooks Lake Champlain. Photo courtesy of the Basin Harbor Club.

Buckley's Great Steaks is located in an historic building built around 1800 in Merrimack, New Hampshire. Photo courtesy of Buckley's Great Steaks.

The Common Man is located in the former Hannah Jack Tavern, an historical building dating back to 1794. Photo courtesy of The Common Man.

Maine's Bar Harbor Inn was designed by architect William Randolph Emerson. Photo by Steve Bauer.

The White Barn Inn's restaurant encompasses two restored barns dating from the 1820s. Photo courtesy of The White Barn Inn.

The Spa at Norwich Inn's Corn and Zucchini Chowder, recipe on page 263. Photo courtesy of The Spa at Norwich Inn.

Hotel Viking is located at the top of Newport's Historic Hill. Photo by Steve Bauer.

The restaurant is the inn's crown jewel. Its exposed beams, hanging chandeliers, sparkling china, and impeccable service are classically romantic. Son and head chef Brill Williams has created a menu concentrating on local fare like rabbit, venison, and quail. Soups are a specialty of the house, and the desserts are often mother's home recipes, like ice cream with dark chocolate butternut sauce. (The sauce is available for purchase at the inn.) The wine list is exceptional and has received the Wine Spectator Grand Award for the past eleven years. There is a selection of 1,285 different wines offering remarkable vintages and labels, all housed in the twenty-eight-thousand-bottle cellar.

Every season is impressive at Sawmill Farm. West Dover is located in the center of the Southern Vermont's Deerfield Valley. Mount Snow, two minutes away, offers skiing and snowboarding on 130 trails. In the summer the mountain offers twenty miles of hiking paths and forty-five miles of mountain biking trails. Guests can enroll in the nearby golf school or play on one of several professional courses in the area. Fisherman can find the only Orvis-endorsed fly fishing school in the Northeast down the road, drawing both novices and veterans to the many trout-fishing sites in the valley. And, of course, there is fall foliage's grand display during September and October.

For these thirty years, running the inn has been a family affair: creator and architect, Rodney; decorator, Ione; now head chef and wine collector, son Brill; and administrator, daughter Bobbie Dee. Each family member's talents flourish within the continuous work in progress.

As Ione says, "The Inn at Sawmill Farm at Mount Snow has survived the events of the years, and we have been growing—not particularly in size because we enjoy the intimacy of a small inn, but we have been active each year with additions and improvements. However, the personality of the inn is still pretty much the same. We still like to think of our inn as unpretentious but curiously sophisticated."

The Inn at Sawmill Farm
Crosstown Road and Route 100
West Dover, VT 05356
(802) 464–8131

 *154*

BATTER

1 1/2 cups all-purpose flour

1 tablespoon paprika

1 teaspoon sea salt

1 teaspoon freshly cracked black
  pepper

12 ounces beer

SHRIMP

1/2 cup all-purpose flour

1/2 teaspoon salt

1/2 teaspoon pepper

12 peeled and deveined raw
  shrimp

2 cups blanched and sliced
  almonds

Vegetable oil

SAUCE

1 tablespoon bottled horseradish

1 teaspoon powdered ginger

Juice of 1 lemon

Juice of 2 oranges

1 cup marmalade

Shrimp in Beer Batter

BATTER

Combine all ingredients and mix until completely smooth and free of lumps.

SHRIMP

Mix the flour, salt, and pepper together. Pat the shrimp dry and toss in the flour mix. Then dip shrimp into the batter holding the shrimp by the tail. Gently shake the excess batter off. Coat shrimp in the almonds and deep fry in vegetable oil until golden brown, usually 2–3 minutes. Do not crowd the fryer and continue until all shrimp are cooked. Drain on paper towels and keep warm.

SAUCE (MAKE IN ADVANCE AND SERVE CHILLED)

Begin by making a paste of the horseradish and the ginger. Take the lemon and orange juices and stir slowly into the paste until smooth. Add the marmalade, mix, and chill. Serve as a dipping sauce for the shrimp.

PLATING

Arrange 3 shrimps per person on a small plate with the pungent sauce. Good with champagne!

YIELD

Serves 4

Sour Cream Coffee Cake

Beat together 2 cups of the sugar and the butter. Add eggs one at a time. Add flour sifted with baking soda, alternating with sour cream, beginning and ending with flour. Add vanilla. Mix together in a separate bowl the remaining cup of sugar, cinnamon, walnuts, and coconut.

Lightly butter and flour a 9" × 13" pan. Pour in batter. Top with sugar mixture and swirl into batter with knife. Bake 1 hour at 350 degrees.

YIELD

Serves 12

3 cups sugar

1 cup butter

4 eggs

3 cups flour

2 teaspoons baking soda

2 cups sour cream

2 teaspoons vanilla extract

2 teaspoons cinnamon

5 tablespoons walnut pieces

5 tablespoons flaked coconut

 *156*

1 cup Grade A or fancy Vermont
   maple syrup

2 tablespoons arrowroot

1 tablespoon cold water

1 1/2 ounces Grand Marnier

2 Granny Smith apples, peeled
   and thinly sliced

4 slices of Vermont smoked ham

4 eggs

4 English muffin halves

Vermont Country Breakfast

Bring syrup to a boil and remove from heat immediately (it will overflow as soon as it starts to boil). Mix arrowroot with cold water until it forms a paste. Add to the syrup to thicken. Simmer for 3 minutes and then add Grand Marnier. Add apple slices to mixture and let simmer on low heat. Heat ham slices in oven or grill slightly until warm. Poach the eggs and toast the muffins.

PLATING

Place poached egg on English muffin on plate. Place ham slice beside muffin and pour syrup and apple mixture over ham.

YIELD

Serves 4

MIDDLEBURY INN
Middlebury

In 1827, Nathan Wood built a brick "public house" first named the Vermont Hotel. In 1852, the inn changed hands and became the Addison House. Darwin Rider bought the property in 1865 when the Civil War ended and proceeded to make many improvements. Service for guests was highlighted by a free carriage to all trains and a complete livery for his guests with their own transportation.

In 1897, Allen Calhoun purchased the Addison House and made extensive renovations, including a three-story addition, new baths, electric lights, steam heat, and a new kitchen and dining room. In 1925, a stock company of local businessmen, the Middlebury Hotel Corporation, bought the Addison House. After additional remodeling, the Addison House reopened in 1927 as the Middlebury Inn.

The most recent addition to the property came in 1968, when twenty modern annex units were added by the Treadway Company. The adjacent Porter Mansion, now part of the Middlebury Inn, is a stately brick home built in 1925 for local merchant Jonathan Wainwright. It is named for the William Porter family that eventually occupied it. With its beautiful curving staircase, fine leaded glass entrance, delicate marble fireplaces, and elaborate moldings, this attractive addition to the inn offers nine Victorian-style guest rooms.

The Middlebury Inn has been in continuous operation as a hotel for over 180 years. With completely refurbished guest rooms, expanded meeting facilities, and the new Waterfalls Day Spa, the Middlebury Inn has entered a new golden era. As one of the most unique historic inns of Vermont, the Middlebury Inn is respectful of the past while offering the comforts and conveniences of the modern world. The Middlebury Inn is like a boutique hotel with its delicious dining, creative event space, attentive guest service, and timeless charm. Afternoon tea and treats while relaxing in classic rockers on the canopied front porch might be the highlight of your afternoon. Complete your day with a great meal in Morgan's Tavern, the inn's fine-dining restaurant.

Among all the historic inns of Vermont, you'll find that the hospitality of the Middlebury Inn lives up to its reputation. You will quickly discover why so many guests return again and again.

 *158*

"Great restaurants are, of course, nothing but mouth brothels. There is no point in going to them if one intends to keep one's belt buckled."

—Frederic Raphael

Middlebury Inn
14 Court Square
Middlebury, VT 05753
(802) 388-4961

Middlebury Inn Popovers

This recipe is scaled down for the home and will hopefully work for you. I would love to say that a recipe so simple is easy, but that never seems to be the case. We use small muffin tins, which you can usually purchase at a Christmas Tree Shop or a Target. Use a little cooking spray to grease them, and they should work pretty well. We spent a lot of time working on this recipe to get a consistent product, and quite honestly it may not work in the home on the first try. Good luck, and, now, it's popover time.

5 eggs

1 1/3 cups milk

2 2/3 tablespoons canola oil

2 cups all-purpose flour

2/3 tablespoon kosher salt

First preheat oven to 350 degrees. If you have an electric mixer, its time to clean the dust off and use it. Mix your eggs, milk, and oil by hand. Then add the flour and salt with the mixer on low. When the ingredients start to bind, turn your mixer up higher and incorporate until the batter is smooth. Coat your muffin tin with cooking spray and fill each cavity to the top. If it overflows a little, you're perfect. Bake for 17 minutes and then rotate 180 degrees. Bake for 17 more minutes, say the Rosary, rub a rabbit's foot five times, look for a penny heads up, and hope for the best. Pick a popover up from the tin. If it's completely browned, you are all set. If the popover is on the pale side, it will collapse, so keep it in the oven for a few minutes longer. This is the hardest part. I hope this recipe brings you fame and fortune. If it does, send me some matchbooks from around the world, and we'll call it even.

 YIELD

1 pint of fresh strawberries

1 cup sour cream

2 cups half-and-half

3 tablespoons brandy

1/4 cup sugar (a little more if you have a sweet tooth)

Pinch of salt

The Middlebury Inn's Famous Strawberry Soup

This recipe was created by a previous chef named Thomas Phelps in 1978. He is an amazing character with incredible stories who still pops his head in a couple of days a week to make sure we are still making the inn's dining as memorable as when he was here.

Place all the ingredients in a blender or use a stick blender and purée until smooth.

This recipe will bring a smile to Tommy every time you make it. Keep it chilled in the fridge; it can always be garnished with more fresh strawberries and a sprig of mint.

YIELD

Serves 6

Spinach Salad with Gorgonzola Dressing, Pistachios, Bacon, and Strawberries

CREAMY GORGONZOLA DRESSING

Use a whisk and mix all the dressing ingredients together in a bowl. Add salt and pepper to taste.

SALAD

Mix the spinach with some of the dressing and pistachios in a bowl. Place some on an individual plate and top them with some of the crumbled bacon, Gorgonzola crumbles, and fresh strawberries.

YIELD

Serves 6

CREAMY GORGONZOLA DRESSING

1 cup mayo

1 1/2 cups buttermilk

1/2 cup crumbled gorgonzola

1 tablespoon garlic, minced

1 tablespoon kosher salt

1 teaspoon cracked black pepper

SALAD

1 bunch of baby spinach (cleaned with stems removed)

1 cup shelled, toasted pistachios

1 cup crumbled bacon

1 cup crumbled gorgonzola or mild Danish blue cheese

2 cups sliced fresh strawberries

OLD TAVERN
AT GRAFTON

Grafton

It is not known when the building was constructed, but Enos Lovell was living in the two-story structure in 1801 when he noted that lodging was needed for travelers. He converted the house into an inn, and that facility is still part of the Old Tavern today. Enos was right, and the inn flourished. In 1823, when Hyman Burgess took over, the inn had doubled in size. The builders were in such a hurry to accommodate the need for space that they failed to match the floor levels, which accounts for the unusual slope in the second- and third-floor corridors.

The tavern had become so important to the town of Grafton that by 1841 the municipal court was held there. At the outbreak of the Civil War, the tavern fell on hard times as ownership changed hands eight times. We know that William and Sophia Stratton owned it for a short period, but little is known about what transpired in the tavern then since most of the records were lost when the schoolhouse where they were stored burned down in 1936. The tavern remained popular, and in 1867 Ulysses S. Grant came while campaigning for his first term as president.

Francis Phelps eventually bought the Old Tavern for $1,700 and sold a half interest to his brother Harlan in 1886. But Harlan got caught up in the fever of the California Gold Rush, although belatedly. He was successful, however, and returned to Grafton with $4,500. Harlan invested every penny in the tavern by adding a third floor and the very popular porches, giving the building the look that has sustained it throughout the years.

The Phelps brothers had created a very popular gathering place. Rudyard Kipling visited in 1892. Other notable guests included Daniel Webster, Oliver Wendell Holmes, Theodore Roosevelt, Woodrow Wilson, and Ralph Waldo Emerson. The tavern was the "in" place for local social events, but it was still primarily a hotel patronized mostly by commercial travelers who knew it as a "good place to stop."

The Phelps brothers died early in the twentieth century, and their widows sold the tavern to Norman Blodgett, who ran it for twenty-seven years. The Great Depression forced Blodgett to sell the property to Harry and Cecelia Dutton, who worked hard to keep the tavern open during that difficult time. In 1937, they sold the inn, and a string of owners followed. During this turmoil, the Homestead property was acquired and added to the tavern's facilities, and the pool area was built.

As guests noted the lack of modern plumbing, private bathrooms, hot and cold running water, and central heating, the tavern went into decline. It could stay open only during the summer months. The cost of adding modern conveniences was considered prohibitive. By 1964, the tavern, in a sad state of repair, was experiencing significant financial challenges. The end was in sight.

During this time, Dean Mathey was a regular visitor to Grafton, and many of his family members owned summer homes in town. But he had more influence over life in Grafton than any other individual throughout the town's history. The Mathey family created the Windham Foundation with the purpose of restoring the village of Grafton.

The Windham Foundation purchased the Old Tavern in 1964, and a year later a major renovation had been completed. The finest modern conveniences were added for guests. A careful hand was used to preserve the famous country-inn character. Today, the Old Tavern boasts forty-six individually appointed rooms with period antiques, including seven suites and rental houses with private baths.

The Old Tavern once again is the center of activity in the historic village of Grafton.

On learning that coffee was considered a slow poison: "I think it must be so,
for I have been drinking it for sixty-five years and I am not dead yet."

—Voltaire

Old Tavern at Grafton
92 Main Street
Grafton, VT 05146
(800) 843-1801

1 tablespoon extra virgin olive oil

1 tablespoon roasted garlic

1 tablespoon capers, rinsed

2 ounces assorted olives

1 tablespoon roasted red peppers, diced

1/4 cup dry white wine

10 mussels

3 large shrimp (quartered)

5 ounces firm textured fish (halibut, swordfish, red snapper)

1 vine-ripened tomato, diced

1/2 cup tomato juice

1/2 cup chicken or vegetable stock

1 tablespoon unsalted butter

1/2 teaspoon freshly ground chili pepper

1/2 teaspoon sea salt

1 tablespoon fennel, diced

1 tablespoon fresh basil, chopped

Sourdough croutons

Mediterranean Bouillabaisse

Combine olive oil, garlic, capers, olives, red peppers, and white wine. Simmer for about 2 minutes. Add mussels and sauté lightly until shells open. Remove mussels and discard any that do not open. Add shrimp and fish and sauté for about a minute. Add diced tomato, tomato juice, stock, butter, chili pepper, salt, fennel, and mussels and bring to a boil. Simmer on medium heat for another 3 minutes. Serve hot and garnish with fresh basil and sourdough croutons.

YIELD

Serves 10

Wild Mushroom and Spinach Risotto with Grafton Smoked Cheddar

Place a thick-bottomed sauce pot on medium-low heat. Sauté shitake, cremini, and oyster mushrooms in three batches with the olive oil and 1 tablespoon butter. Cook to golden brown. Add splash of balsamic vinegar to caramelize each batch of mushrooms. Set aside cooked mushrooms.

In the same pot, on medium-low heat, heat 1 tablespoon butter and 1 tablespoon olive oil. Add onion and shallot and sauté until caramelized. Add 2 ounces of the white wine to deglaze.

Add Arborio rice with 2 tablespoons olive oil and stir well. Add 6 ounces miso stock, 2 ounces wine, and 1 teaspoon butter, continually stirring the rice. Keep repeating the stock, wine, and butter combination until all broth is absorbed (approximately 20–25 minutes). Cook to al dente.

Add spinach until wilted, then the roasted garlic, Grafton cheddar, and Parmesan. Add mushrooms and season dish with salt, pepper, and lemon zest.

YIELD

Serves 6–8

1/2 pound shitake mushrooms

1/2 pound cremini mushrooms

1/2 pound oyster mushrooms

2 tablespoons olive oil

1 tablespoon butter

Splash of balsamic vinegar

1 tablespoon butter

1 tablespoon extra virgin olive oil

1 large sweet onion, thinly julienned

1 shallot, finely chopped

1 bottle white wine, Chardonnay

2 cups Arborio rice

2 tablespoons olive oil

1 1/2 quarts miso broth (combine yellow miso and hot water)

1 teaspoon butter

1/2 pound baby spinach

1 bulb roasted garlic, chopped

6 ounces Grafton maple-smoked cheddar, grated

1/4 cup Parmesan cheese

Sea salt and freshly ground black pepper to taste

1 teaspoon lemon zest

Roasted Butternut Squash and Sweet Potato Bisque

2 pounds butternut squash, peeled and diced (1-inch cubes)

1 pound sweet potatoes, peeled and diced (1-inch cubes)

2 ounces maple syrup

4 ounces unsalted butter, divided, melted

1 teaspoon ground cinnamon

1 garlic bulb

2 ounces extra virgin olive oil

2 large sweet onions, thinly sliced

2 shallots, thinly sliced

4 ounces sherry

1 cup apple cider

1 cup heavy cream

2 quarts chicken or vegetable stock

1 tablespoon fresh thyme, finely chopped

1 teaspoon ground allspice

Salt and pepper to taste

Mix squash and sweet potatoes in bowl with maple syrup, melted butter, and cinnamon. Place on baking pan and cover. Take garlic bulb, coat with olive oil, and wrap in foil. Place the baking pan with the squash, sweet potatoes, and wrapped garlic bulb in a 350-degree oven for 30 minutes. Upon completion, pull out all roasted garlic cloves and set aside. Discard garlic peels. Set aside cooked squash and sweet potatoes. Add oil and butter to a large, thick-bottomed saucepan. Add onions and shallots and sauté on low heat until lightly caramelized. Add sherry to deglaze the pan. Add apple cider and simmer for 5 minutes. Add baked squash/sweet potatoes and add cream, stock, thyme, and allspice. Simmer for approximately 10 minutes. Purée in blender until smooth. Add salt and freshly ground pepper to taste and serve.

YIELD

1 gallon

New Hampshire

BEDFORD VILLAGE INN

Bedford

The Bedford Village Inn and Restaurant was built around a farmhouse that dates from Bedford's agricultural past. "The Gordon Farm," as the BVI grounds are called in early town records, was originally part of a large parcel granted to one John McLaughlin, the first town clerk of Bedford. A savvy and well-placed speculator, McLaughlin subdivided his parcel, selling a fifty-acre corner to neighbor Samuel Gordon. John Gordon, Sam's younger brother, cleared the land in 1774 and subsequently raised most of his fourteen children at the inn.

Josiah, eldest son of John Gordon, joined the Continental army at the start of the Revolutionary War, wearing a linen shirt sewn by his mother from flax grown and woven on the farm. Upon his triumphant return, Josiah became a gentleman farmer and businessman and built the present federal farmhouse in 1810. The Beard Farm next door supported a tenant of note during the early 1800s: Mr. Zaccheus Greeley, father of Horace Greeley, who attended the #1 School located near the corner of Bedford Center and Chandler roads at the time.

In 1832 a "granddaughter of John Gordon" married Dr. Peter P. Woodbury, who practiced medicine in Bedford for many years and helped write an early history of the town in 1850. The Gordon Farm was passed between the Gordons and Woodburys until 1940, when Judge Peter Woodbury sold the place to Henry and Olga Wheeler. The Wheeler family raised prized Shetland ponies on the site until the construction of Route 101 in 1953 cut the pasturage off from the farmhouse. New Hampshire built a pony-sized underpass beneath the highway, but it proved inconvenient for the Wheelers and their herd, so they moved west to Jaffrey, New Hampshire, the following year.

The Wheeler family left both halves of the spread to "gentleman farmers" Ralph and Sybil Fletcher, who subsequently sold the old pasturage on the opposite side of Route 101. During these years the original farm had grown from 50 to nearly 350 acres. With the decline in farming and the increased activity in residential and infrastructure development, the original farm estate was preserved at five and a half acres by 1980. In 1981 the "farm" was purchased with the intention of renovating the house as a restaurant and the old livestock barn as an inn.

Over the next three years, the owners worked with a coalition of like-minded citizens and Bedford Planning Board members to save Fletcher Farm by rezoning the property for use as a "Class

A Inn and Restaurant." Two years of delicate preservation work and substantial new construction began in the summer of 1984 with the result that the restaurant opened in August 1985 and the inn opened in October 1986.

The Bedford Village Inn and Restaurant stands on the entry to Bedford as testimony of what can be accomplished by combining the commitment of many townspeople, the high standards of a skilled architect and builder, and the constant attention to detail of a talented staff. The melding of old and new blends grace with function and defines the special appeal of the Bedford Village Inn.

Jack and Andrea Carnevale purchased the Bedford Village Inn in 1990, and throughout their ownership, the inn has garnered local and national recognition for its elegant charm and world-class accommodations and cuisine.

Bedford Village Inn
2 Olde Bedford Way
Bedford, NH 03110
(603) 472-2001
(800) 852-1166

Roasted Organic Pumpkin Bisque with Toasted Pepitas and Pumpkin Seed Oil

1 small pumpkin

2 onions, small-diced and sweated in 2 tablespoons butter in 8-quart soup pot

2 tablespoons butter

2 quarts chicken stock

1 tablespoon Madras curry powder

2 cups heavy cream

Salt and pepper

1/4 cup pumpkin seeds

1 tablespoon canola oil

1 ounce pumpkin seed oil, optional

Cut pumpkin in half and roast seed side down on a cookie sheet at 375 degrees for 25–35 minutes. Sweat onions in 8-quart soup pot in 2 tablespoons of butter. Once pumpkin has cooled, remove the seeds, peel the skin, and add to the soup pot. Cover with 2 quarts of chicken stock and 1 tablespoon of curry powder. Bring pot to a boil and simmer for 45 minutes. Add 2 cups of heavy cream, bring back to a boil, then turn off.

Next, purée soup smooth in a blender; do this in small batches, or you run the risk of wearing hot soup. While blending the soup, add each batch back into a soup pot and place back on the stove to reheat. Season with salt and pepper.

Toast pumpkin seeds in a sauté pan with 1 tablespoon of canola oil for garnish.

Pumpkin seed oil can be purchased at a specialty food store. The type from Austria is the best.

YIELD

Serves 4

Apple-and-Leek-Stuffed Niman Ranch Pork Chop

Wrapped in prosciutto with maple-whipped sweet potatoes, black mission fig jam, and sautéed wax beans

FIG JAM

Slice dried Black Mission figs lengthwise to 1/8 inch thick. Place figs in a stainless steel saucepan with balsamic and red wine vinegar and sugar. Bring this to a quick boil on the stove top and then lower the heat until the item is at a simmer. Slowly reduce this jam until liquid around the figs reaches at a syrupy consistency. Jam is done.

PORK CHOPS WITH APPLE AND LEEK STUFFING

Remove green top from the leek and then cut in half. Next, cut the leek into 1/4-inch half moons and place in a bowl of cold water to remove any soil. Peel Granny Smith apples, slice in half, and cut into 1/4-inch wedges. In a sauté pan large enough to hold all the items, melt butter with sage and thyme. Once butter is melted add the apples and leeks (removed from the water). Cook the ingredients on medium heat until soft. Cool stuffing and remove thyme and sage.

To stuff pork, cut pockets in the center of each chop on its side (like a book) and place cool stuffing inside. Wrap each chop with two pieces of prosciutto.

FIG JAM

1 cup dried Black Mission figs

1/2 cup balsamic vinegar

1/2 cup red wine vinegar

1/2 cup sugar

PORK CHOPS WITH APPLE AND LEEK STUFFING

1 leek

2 Granny Smith apples

2 tablespoons butter

1 leaf of sage

1 sprig of thyme

4 large pork chops

8 thinly sliced pieces of prosciutto

1 tablespoon canola oil

WHIPPED SWEET
POTATOES

2 sweet potatoes

1 cup butter, melted

2 tablespoons maple syrup

WAX BEANS

1/2 pound wax beans

1 tablespoon butter

1 tablespoon fresh parsley,
    chopped

1 tablespoon shallots, chopped

To cook the chops, first place a large sauté pan on the stove at high heat and add oil. Then place each chop in the hot pan and sear until brown. Place the pan with chops into 375-degree oven for 15–20 minutes until chops are cooked to medium.

WHIPPED SWEET POTATOES

Peel sweet potatoes, cut into pieces, and place in a pot. Cover with water, bring to a boil, and simmer until soft. Remove potatoes from water and place in food processor with melted butter and maple syrup. Purée smooth and then place in pot on stove to keep warm.

WAX BEANS

Cook in salted boiling water for 3 minutes, remove, and shock. Reheat on stove in a sauté pan with butter, parsley, and shallots.

YIELD

Serves 4

BUCKLEY'S
GREAT STEAKS
Merrimack

On a highway between revolutionary Boston and Concord, New Hampshire, Isaac Riddle built a tavern circa 1790. The area was known then as Souhegan Village, on the banks of the Souhegan River. The river got its name more than three hundred years ago from the Penacook Indians, who hunted and fished the area. Roughly translated, the name Souhegan means "river of the plains."

Riddle's Tavern, as it was known, was a place of refreshment and relaxation, a refuge from the "highway" in the late 1700s. Hand-cut and notched in the nearby woods, the tavern's posts and beams have stood square for over two hundred years.

Yankee ingenuity employed in the engineering strategically placed the softer Eastern pine in lieu of the firm Douglas fir center beams under the second-floor ballroom to give the dance floor a natural spring for the popular Friday night mixers. People came from as far as fifty miles away by stagecoach for the Friday dancing and festivities.

A swinging partition wall in the upstairs ballroom lifted to reveal an alcove in which the orchestra would set up to play music. The warm, natural orange glow of the pumpkin pine single-plank wainscoting still frames the dining room and the eight fireplaces. The foundation is made of granite slabs twelve to fourteen inches thick.

While climbing the spiral stairs during his stay at the tavern nearly half a century later, President Andrew Jackson paused a moment to give the cook his fried-donut recipe for the morning meal.

Riddle, a prominent business man, also owned the Souhegan Nail, Cotton and Woolen Manufacturing Mill across the road and the general store next door. The arrival of the railroad brought the tavern into several years of dormancy and disrepair. Between 1940 and 1978, it functioned as a residence in which the Nute family raised ten children.

In 1895 Gordon Woodbury purchased the mill across the road for the Merrimack Shoe Company and brought the tavern back to life as a boarding home for the hands working at his shoe shop. Over the years the tavern has served as an executive's home and a private residence; it was finally renovated to its original purpose as a place of hospitality in 1978. Today it is a fine-dining restaurant.

Buckley's Great Steaks was opened in the original Riddle's Tavern in 2005. Several rooms are dedicated to providing fine steaks and other fare, but the watering hole is still called Riddle's Tavern.

Buckley's Great Steaks
438 Daniel Webster Highway
Merrimack, NH 03054
(603) 424-0995

Sugar-Cured New York Sirloin

Mix brown sugar, garlic, and cayenne until fully incorporated. Spread a 1/2 cup of the mixture on the bottom of a baking dish and press the steaks into the cure. Spread the remaining cure on top of the steaks and press to adhere. Cover and refrigerate overnight or for up to 24 hours.

Grill over indirect medium-high heat until desired doneness is reached.

❧ YIELD ❧

Serves 6–8

2 cups lightly packed brown
   sugar

2 teaspoons fresh garlic, minced

1/4 teaspoon cayenne pepper

4 fourteen-ounce choice
   New York sirloins

3 Idaho potatoes, peeled and halved crosswise

2 slices thick-cut bacon, diced to 1/4 inch

2 tablespoons whole butter

1/4 cup green onion, sliced

Salt and pepper to taste

Rosti Potatoes

Boil potatoes until fork tender and cool immediately. Once cool, shred on a grater or with a food processor. Crisp diced bacon in a skillet and render 1/2 of the fat. Add 1 tablespoon of butter, sprinkle shredded potatoes in one layer over the crisp bacon, and add the green onion. Cook over medium-high heat for 4–6 minutes, taking care not to stir the potatoes. When potatoes are golden brown, flip the them "pancake style" onto the other side and add butter as needed. Continue cooking until potatoes are a crisp golden brown. Season with salt and pepper to taste.

YIELD

Serves 6

Oven-Baked Oysters

Place prosciutto strips on a flat work surface. Starting at one end, place 1 oyster, covered with 1 ounce drained spinach and 3–4 strips sun-dried tomato. Wrap prosciutto around oyster and spinach and place in a rinsed shell. Place oysters in an oven-safe dish and drizzle white wine over them. Bake at 425 degrees for approximately 5 minutes. Cover each oyster with hollandaise sauce and serve.

YIELD

Serves 4

2 slices prosciutto, thinly sliced

8 oysters, shucked, shells rinsed

1/2 pound sautéed spinach, drained

6 sun-dried tomato halves, cut into thin strips

1 ounce white wine

2 ounces hollandaise sauce

CAFÉ LAFAYETTE DINNER TRAIN
North Woodstock

The Café Lafayette Dinner Train calls itself "the restaurant with the constantly changing view." That is certainly the case as it winds its way through the fields and forests of the Pemigewasset River in the heart of the White Mountain Region of New Hampshire. In operation since 1989, the Café Lafayette Dinner Train is under the ownership of Lance Burak and Leslie Holloway.

Approximately twenty moving dinner trains travel through North America, making the Café Lafayette Dinner Train a very unique and unusual attraction in the Lincoln and North Woodstock area.

Although the operation is relatively new, the cars that make up the dinner train certainly are not. Car #221, "Indian Waters," is a beautifully restored 1924 Pullman dining car originally built for, and operated on, the New York Central. The car was rebuilt in the mid-1980s from the trucks up in the Winnipesaukee Rail Yard by skilled craftsmen and the previous owner. It operated for two years on the Winnipesaukee Railroad and was later moved to Lincoln in the summer of 1988. It then operated for one year on the Hobo Railroad before it was purchased by the current owners of the Café Lafayette Dinner Train. Lance Burak and Leslie Holloway continued to operate the "Indian Waters" from the rail station until the summer of 1998 when the Café Lafayette Dinner Train was moved to its new location at the "Eagle's Nest."

Car #2221, known today as the "Granite Eagle," was originally built for the Missouri-Pacific Railroad. It operated from St. Louis, Missouri, to San Antonio, Texas, in the mid-1950s on the "Texas Eagle" line. It was later acquired by the Illinois Railroad and run on train #1, one of the most famous trains in American music, if not history, "The City of New Orleans." Burak and Holloway purchased this unusual dome car in Pittsburgh, Kansas, in the late fall of 1995. It was brought across the United States by rail and refurbished in the engine house of the Hobo Railroad during the winter of 1996. Leslie, Lance, and their staff, along with a friend, made the impossible happen. They took only six months to rebuild the exterior steel, redesign and restore the interior, install new windows, and give this splendid car a royal blue and white paint job. Upon completion of their renovation, they renamed it the "Granite Eagle."

The "Algonquin," car #3207, is a 1953 X-CNR Café Coach purchased in 1995 from the Canadian government. It was used as a storage car for several years, but the need for a dance car to celebrate New Year's Eve 2000 arose. The refurbishment began in the summer of 1999, with efforts completed in time for Y2K festivities. Now, its spacious and open interior makes it a great gathering place for private parties and corporate outings.

When you come, visit the nearby Kancamagus Scenic Byway only minutes from Clark's Trading Post, Lost River Gorge, Whales Tale Water Park, Loon Mountain Resort, and the legendary Woodstock Inn. While in the area, you may also go to Franconia Notch State Park, home to the Flume Gorge, the Cannon Mountain Tram Ride, and the famous "Old Man of the Mountain" site where you can see what is left after the rock formation collapsed. A trip on the Café Lafayette Dinner Train and a visit to North Woodstock will be a memorable vacation.

Café Lafayette Dinner Train
P.O. Box 8
North Woodstock, NH 03262
(603) 745-3500
(800) 699-3501

1/4 pound butter

1/2 pound pecan halves

1/4 teaspoon salt

1 pint fresh blueberries

Honey or maple syrup to taste

Applesauce to taste

Blueberry Pecan Salsa

Melt butter in sauté pan over medium heat. Add pecan halves and toss to coat with butter. Sprinkle with the salt. Lightly brown the pecans and remove from heat. While still hot, combine with blueberries, taking care to avoid crushing the berries.

Add honey or maple syrup to desired consistency. Applesauce can be substituted for some or all of the honey to achieve desired taste or consistency.

Salsa may be gently reheated, but do not simmer or boil. Serve at room temperature.

YIELD

1 quart

Pork Tenderloin with Blueberry Pecan Salsa

After trimming tenderloin, marinate for 4–12 hours in your favorite marinade. Pork can be grilled or roasted in a hot oven at 425 degrees. Finish to medium rare or to taste.

PLATING

Slice into medallions approximately 1/2 inch thick. Fan out onto a hot plate and top with blueberry pecan salsa. Garnish with fresh sage leaves.

YIELD

Serves 6–8

Whole pork tenderloin, trimmed

Pork marinade

Blueberry pecan salsa (see p. 180)

Fresh sage leaves

CAKE

9 eggs

3 cups sugar

2 1/2 cups flour

1 tablespoon baking soda

2 teaspoons cinnamon

2 cups canned pumpkin

FILLING

1/2 pound butter

1 1/2 pounds cream cheese

3 cups confectioners' sugar

1 1/2 teaspoons vanilla extract

Splash of maple syrup

Pumpkin Spice Roll

From the kitchen of Jane Holloway, mother of one of the owners of the Café Lafayette Dinner Train

CAKE

Beat eggs and sugar until thick and pale in color. Sift together flour, soda, and cinnamon. Add pumpkin to beaten eggs and fold into flour mixture. Pour mixture onto a full sheet pan lined with baker's parchment or wax paper. Bake at 375 degrees for 12–15 minutes.

FILLING

Soften butter and cream cheese. Combine softened butter, cream cheese, and sugar until smooth. Add vanilla and maple syrup.

Completely cool cake and spread filling from edge to edge while still in sheet pan. Lift up one of the short edges of the cake and roll. Sprinkle with sugar.

Serve with homemade whipped cream or French vanilla ice cream.

⚓ YIELD ⚓

Serves 10

CANTERBURY SHAKER VILLAGE

Canterbury

Canterbury Shaker Village was established in 1792 when followers of founder Mother Ann Lee formed their seventh community in Canterbury, New Hampshire. The village, which remained prominent for two hundred years, has operated exclusively as a museum since 1992, when the last Shaker sister in residence, Ethel Hudson, died. The few remaining Shakers live at the Shaker Village in Sabbathday Lake, Maine. At the height of its glory in the 1850s, three hundred people lived and worked in over one hundred buildings on three thousand acres at Canterbury Shaker Village.

The religious group known today as the Shakers was formed in eighteenth-century England near Manchester when dissidents from various religions, including English Quakers and Methodists, formed a religious society based on prophetic doctrine. The group, formally called the United Society of Believers in Christ's Second Appearing, was known as the Shaking Quakers, or Shakers, because of members' unusual habit of making odd dancelike moves during worship ceremonies.

The Shakers immigrated to the United States in 1774 after Mother Ann proclaimed that she had received a vision from God that he had prepared a place for them in America. They eventually established eighteen self-contained communities from Maine to Kentucky with a population in 1850 of almost four thousand members. Canterbury Shaker Village is one of the oldest, most typical, and most completely preserved of the Shaker villages. The village contains the only intact, first-generation meetinghouse, built in 1792, and dwelling house, built in 1793, in their original locations. Overall, the Shakers were the most successful communal society in American history.

The Shakers' revolutionary Christianity shocked many of their contemporaries. They challenged almost every mainstream ideal of American society during their time. Shakers believed in community ownership, pacifism, dancing in worship, equality of the sexes, celibacy, and living simply. Most Protestants of the day found that bringing dancing, whirling, and clapping into a sacred space and elevating it above the word of God, spoken by an ordained minister, was sacrilegious. But to the Shakers, the dancing signified a communal, not individual, relationship with God, which was a powerful symbol of the Shaker cultural system.

Despite the monastic characteristics of their communities, the Shakers were not primarily a contemplative religious society. According to founder Mother Ann Lee, the Shakers devoted their

"hands to work and hearts to God." Although they believed in community ownership, they were aggressive entrepreneurs, launching industry after industry, developing and adopting new technologies, and reinvesting the earnings into community enterprises to encourage even more growth and productivity. At their height, they were highly successful in competing with the outside world.

By the 1830s the industrious and skilled Shakers at Canterbury were rich in buildings, land, cash, wood lots, livestock, produce, and community possessions. The Shaker "brand" quickly became known for quality, integrity, and reliability. Shakers cared for the poor and used resources and profit for social good. One of their most enduring legacies is the quality and style of Shaker furniture. Their designs have been copied and sold on both sides of the Atlantic through IKEA megastores.

Today, the museum at Canterbury interprets two hundred years of Shaker life through exhibits, buildings, gardens, programs, and tours. The museum has an enviable collection of Shaker objects, manuscripts, and photographs, along with surviving architecture from all periods of its history. Canterbury Shaker Village is a unique resource for learning about Shaker architectural intent and early Shaker community planning and design, as well as the many periods of Shaker life. The postcard-perfect setting hosts tens of thousands of visitors each year, making it one of New Hampshire's most popular cultural attractions. The recipes that follow are from the Shaker Table restaurant in the village.

Canterbury Shaker Village
288 Shaker Road
Canterbury, NH 03224
(603) 783-9511

Shaker Cornmeal Pancakes

This is a great variation on the traditional pancake. Cornmeal adds a wonderful taste and texture not found in ordinary pancakes. This is a staple on the Shaker Table's brunch menu.

In a medium bowl, whisk eggs until incorporated.

Add buttermilk and sugar.

Stir until well blended.

Add all baking powder, flour, yellow cornmeal, and salt until well blended.

Cook on a well-greased nonstick pan or griddle.

3 farm-fresh eggs

3 cups buttermilk

3 tablespoons sugar

1 1/2 tablespoons baking powder

1 1/2 cups all-purpose flour

2 cups yellow cornmeal

1/2 teaspoon salt

❧ YIELD ❧

Serves 4

FILLING

1 whole roasting chicken
    (4 pounds)

1 gallon low-sodium chicken
    broth

2 pounds onions, diced

1 pound carrots, diced

1 pound celery, diced

1 pound butter

4 bay leaves

4 cloves garlic, minced

2 teaspoons thyme

2 teaspoons marjoram

3 cups flour

2 cups white wine

1 pound peeled potatoes, diced

Salt and pepper to taste

CRUST

2 1/2 cups flour

1 1/2 teaspoons salt

3 tablespoons baking powder

1 tablespoon sugar

1 pint heavy cream

Chicken Pot Pie with Cream Biscuit Crust

FILLING

Put chicken and chicken broth into a large stockpot and simmer over medium heat for approximately 4 hours. Strain and save broth. Let chicken cool slightly, remove all the meat, and reserve.

Sautee onions, carrots, and celery in butter until soft. Add bay leaves, garlic, thyme, and marjoram and sauté 2 more minutes. Add flour and stir until there is no more white showing. Add wine and stir until incorporated. Add reserved chicken broth, stir well, reduce heat to medium, and simmer for 30 minutes. Add diced potatoes and simmer an additional 30 minutes until potatoes are tender. Adjust seasoning with salt and pepper. Add diced cooked chicken. Cool.

CRUST

Preheat oven to 375 degrees.

In a large mixing bowl, sift together the dry ingredients.

In another bowl, whip cream to stiff peaks.

Gently fold the whipped cream into the flour, salt, baking powder, and sugar.

Put dough on a lightly floured surface and knead until all the cream and flour are well incorporated.

Roll to about 1/2-inch thickness.

ASSEMBLY

Fill casserole dish 3/4 with pot pie filling.

Cut dough to fit the dish you are using.

Gently lay the dough on top of the pot pie.

Bake for approximately 30 minutes, or until golden brown and bubbly.

≁ YIELD ≁

Serves 8

3 pounds russet potatoes, peeled

1/2 stick butter

2/3 cup sour cream

3 eggs

1 cup scallions, sliced

2 cups smoked ham, finely diced

1/2 cup Parmesan cheese, grated

1 cup Panko bread crumbs

Kosher salt and pepper

BREADING

1 cup flour

3 eggs beaten with 3 tablespoons milk

2 cups Panko bread crumbs, mixed with 2 teaspoons fresh herbs, chopped

2 cups vegetable oil for frying

Ham and Potato Croquettes

Boil potatoes in salted water until tender, about 45 minutes. Drain well.

In the bowl of a mixer, with the paddle attachment, mix potatoes with butter and sour cream. Add eggs, scallions, smoked ham, Parmesan, and bread crumbs and blend well.

Form into 3-ounce patties and chill for 3 hours until firm. Coat with flour, then egg wash, then breadcrumb mixture.

Heat 2 cups of oil to 360 degrees in a cast iron skillet over medium-high heat. Fry the croquettes for about 2 minutes per side, or until golden brown. Sprinkle with kosher salt and pepper. Serve immediately.

YIELD

Serves 12

THE COMMON MAN
Merrimack

If you have been in New England for any length of time, you have probably seen, or even dined at, a Common Man restaurant. The first Common Man opened in Ashland, New Hampshire, in November 1971. It only held thirty-five people, but lines formed quickly. The enthusiasm of proprietor Alex Ray could not be contained. There wasn't a waiting area or lounge, so patrons would line up outside—even in the winter—and wait for an open table. The cook said he used to run out of the kitchen and peek around the building to see how long the line was. People waiting would look in the door and see customers ordering more coffee. The whisper would then run down the line of waiting people, "Oh, nuts, they're having more coffee."

In 1974, Alex was able to convert the carriage house behind the restaurant into more dining space. Patrons still had to wait, but it was now a warm place. By 1977, Alex and his young family had moved out of the rooms above the main restaurant and converted the space into the Step Above Lounge, which is now a local landmark.

In October 1985, Alex purchased the old Pollard family home in Lincoln, New Hampshire. He and his crew moved an old barn to the site and attached it to the house for additional dining space. It took just forty-seven days from the date of purchase before the second Common Man restaurant opened for business.

In 1987, Alex bought the old Howard Johnson's restaurant in Concord, New Hampshire. He renovated the building, keeping the old-style counter service and turning the rest of the place into a real, old-fashioned, 1950s-style restaurant called the Capital City Diner.

Over the years, Alex has created the Tilt'n Diner in Tilton, the Italian Farmhouse in Plymouth, the Squam Seafood Company in Holderness, the Inn at Bay Point and Boathouse Grille Restaurant in downtown Meredith, the Boathouse Grille in Lago, the Common Man restaurant in Windham, the Common Man Company Store in Ashland, Chase House and Camp restaurant in downtown Meredith, Town Docks in Meredith, and the Lakehouse Grille in Church Landing at Mill Falls in Meredith.

Alex replaced the Capital City Diner in Concord with a Common Man restaurant in 2000. The old structure was completely removed to make way for a New England town home and barn. In

2001, the Common Man in Lincoln was burned by an arsonist, but Alex and his staff rebuilt it in just sixty days.

In 2001 and 2002, the Common Man family took a sixty-thousand-square-foot defunct mill in Plymouth and, retaining 90 percent of the original building, ingeniously transformed it into the thirty-seven-room Common Man Inn & Spa and Foster's Boiler Room restaurant. Renovating historic properties got into Alex's blood. In 2005, he renovated the historic building in Merrimack that had housed the Hannah Jack's restaurant. The newest of the Common Man restaurants was born in the oldest building.

Alex explains why they are popular: "Well, ever since we opened the Common Man in Ashland in 1971, we've been serving Great American Fare—that's lots of fresh seafood, our famous 'Roast Prime Rib,' Country Meat Loaf, hearty soups and sandwiches . . . you get the picture. Or head upstairs, sink into one of our comfortable couches and order some of our lighter fare. So that's what we have planned for our newest restaurant in Merrimack . . . good honest food that is served fresh daily." All Common Man restaurants operate on a first come, first served basis.

"Travel is fatal to prejudice, bigotry, and narrow-mindedness."

—Mark Twain

The Common Man
304 Daniel Webster Highway
Merrimack, NH 03054
(603) 429-3463

The Common Man Crab Cakes

Voted Best of New Hampshire five years in a row by readers of New Hampshire Magazine!

CRAB CAKES

Drain all liquid from crabmeat.

Mix all ingredients together.

Form cakes into 4-ounce portions about 1 inch thick.

Bake on greased pan in 350-degree oven for approximately 8 minutes.

Flip cakes and bake another 6 minutes, or until they reach desired crispness. Cakes should be crispy on the outside and fluffy on the inside. Top or garnish plate with chive horseradish aioli.

CHIVE HORSERADISH AIOLI

Put all ingredients in food processor and purée until smooth. Or purée chives and mix well with other ingredients.

YIELD
Serves 6

CRAB CAKES

2 1/2 pounds rock crabmeat

1/2 cup red bell pepper, diced

1/2 cup green bell pepper, diced

1/2 cup onion, diced

2 1/2 cups celery, diced

3 eggs

1 tablespoon Tabasco sauce

1 tablespoon Worcestershire sauce

3/4 cup mayonnaise

1/2 cup Panko bread crumbs

1/2 cup Italian bread crumbs

CHIVE HORSERADISH AIOLI

1 ounce chives, chopped

1 1/2 cups mayonnaise

1/2 ounce lemon juice

1/4 cup sour cream

2 tablespoons Dijon mustard

2 tablespoons horseradish

1/4 teaspoon thyme

1 teaspoon sugar

Dash salt and pepper

Baked Macaroni and Cheese

1 pound elbow macaroni

1 pound sharp cheddar cheese, grated

1/2 cup Parmesan cheese

1/2 cup bread crumbs

SAUCE

1/4 pound butter

1/4 cup onions, chopped

4 ounces flour

4 cups milk

3 cups half-and-half

1 tablespoon salt

1/4 tablespoon white pepper

1/4 tablespoon ground black pepper

Cook pasta in boiling salted water until tender.

Separately, melt butter in a heavy-bottomed sauce pot.

Add onions and cook on low for 5 minutes.

Add flour and cook on low for another 5 minutes.

Slowly whisk in milk, half-and-half, salt, white pepper, and black pepper and simmer on low for about 15 minutes until the sauce has thickened.

Mix together cooked pasta, sauce, and 1 pound grated sharp cheddar cheese.

Place in a baking dish and top with 1/2 cup bread crumbs mixed with 1/2 cup Parmesan cheese.

Bake in 350-degree oven for about 30 minutes until top is golden brown and the sides begin to bubble.

YIELD

Serves 6–8

Uncommon Baked Apple

The Common Man's signature dessert

Peel and core Macintosh apples.

Mix together in a bowl sugar, flour, cinnamon, and nutmeg.

Melt stick of margarine and dip each apple in the margarine until covered. Roll apple in the sugar and flour mixture until covered. Place in baking dish.

In separate pan, prepare apple glaze by mixing together pancake syrup, water, nutmeg, cinnamon, lemon juice, and brown sugar. Bring mixture to a boil and then pour over apples in baking dish.

Bake apples at 350 degrees for 20 minutes, or until they are soft.

Serve warm with a scoop of vanilla ice cream.

YIELD
Serves 4

4 Macintosh apples

1/2 cup sugar

2 tablespoons flour

1 teaspoon cinnamon

1 teaspoon nutmeg

1 stick margarine

1 gallon of vanilla ice cream

APPLE GLAZE

1/2 cup pancake syrup

1/4 cup water

1/2 teaspoon nutmeg

1/2 teaspoon cinnamon

2 tablespoons lemon juice

3 tablespoons brown sugar

EAGLE MOUNTAIN HOUSE

Jackson

When Capt. John Smith of England, and later of Virginia, sailed along the New Hampshire coast, he was very impressed with the area. He called it North Virginia, but King James changed the name to New England and then gave a land grant to Capt. John Mason. When Mason sent representatives to establish a fishing colony, they renamed it New Hampshire after Mason's home county in England.

Industry flourished, and numerous travelers came to the area. In 1879 the original Eagle Mountain House, a New England farmhouse accommodating up to twelve guests, opened under the ownership of Cyrus Gale. The inn was soon expanded to two buildings accommodating 125 guests, who enjoyed spectacular views, rural surroundings, and great sports such as skiing, hiking, snowshoeing, sledding, and trout fishing. The barn on the property is original to this period, as is the carriage house ballroom, which first held horse carts and carriages, was later used for automobiles, and now handles banquet functions for up to 225 people.

The main inn was completely destroyed by fire in 1915, but it took less than a year before the Eagle Mountain House was rebuilt and reopened. The new inn boasted a 280-foot verandah and 125 rooms with 100 full baths.

Famous photographer Clifton Church documented many scenes around the original inn and stayed as a guest even after the fire. The "Jackson" sign hanging on the covered bridge was a gift from Mr. Church in the 1920s. His pictures of the inn are displayed in the Eagle Landing Tavern.

In 1931, the son of Cyrus Gale turned the farmland and cow pasture in front of the inn into the Eagle Mountain House Golf Course by Arthur Gale. Today, it is one of the most beautiful nine-hole mountain courses in New England with three elevated tee shots along the nationally protected Wildcat River.

The golf course had a real purpose during the winter. In 1937, well-known ski instructor Beno Rybizka supervised the first organized skiing activity in the Mount Washington Valley on the ninth hole of the Eagle Mountain House Golf Course. He had come from Austria to start Carroll Reed's Eastern Slope Region Ski School headquartered in the Wildcat Tavern in Jackson Village.

Mr. and Mrs. Orin Chadbourn took over the inn in 1958 and installed the swimming pool. They owned the inn until 1973, when an owners' association was formed to manage the property.

The association totally restored the inn in 1986, and it now offers ninety-three guest rooms and suites, each privately owned. The association strives to maintain the historic nature of the inn, while creating a year-round resort for the public's enjoyment.

The Eagle Mountain House joined the National Register of Historic Places in 1991, and in 1995 it was listed by the National Trust for Historic Preservation as one of the Historic Hotels of America.

Eagle Mountain House
179 Carter Notch Road
Jackson, NH 03846
(603) 383-9111

1 can roasted red peppers

3 cups mayo

3 7-ounce cans crab meat

3 cups Panko crumbs

1 tablespoon Worcestershire sauce

1 teaspoon Tabasco

2 tablespoons Old Bay

1/4 cup lemon juice

Crab Cakes

Combine mayo and roasted peppers in a food processor. In a large bowl, mix crab meat, bread crumbs, Worcestershire sauce, Tabasco, Old Bay, and lemon juice together and portion with 4-ounce ice-cream scoop. Cover crab cakes with more Panko crumbs.

YIELD

Serves 6

Broccoli Salad

Blend the vinegar, mayo, and sugar with the onion to make the dressing. Dressing may be prepared the day before and refrigerated.

Fold the broccoli, walnuts, and raisins into the dressing and blend well. Serve well chilled.

You may want to substitute dried cranberries for the raisins.

⚬⟊ YIELD ⟊⚬

3 1/2 cups

1 tablespoon white vinegar

1/2 cup mayo

2 tablespoons sugar

1/4 cup Spanish onion, minced

2 cups fresh broccoli, chopped
(use the stem and the florets of broccoli)

1/4 cup walnuts, chopped

1/4 cup raisins*

EF LANE HOTEL
Keene

The community of Keene was originally established as Upper Ashuelot in 1735 by colonial governor Jonathan Belcher, who gave grants of land to soldiers who had fought in the war against Canada. Settled after 1736, it was intended to be a fort town protecting the province of Massachusetts Bay during the French and Indian Wars.

As more settlers moved into New England, controversies arose as to where the proper boundaries should be drawn. The provinces of Massachusetts and New Hampshire had a continuing disagreement as to where their borders lay, but the issue was finally settled by King George II in 1740. The area of Keene was part of this dispute, but the king decided that the true boundary would be about ten miles south, leaving the new township far within the limits of New Hampshire.

During the third of the French and Indian Wars, also known as King George's War, Indians attacked and burned the village. The colonists fled to safety but returned to build the town again in the early 1750s. In 1753, Gov. Benning Wentworth granted landowners the land included in Upper Ashuelot's original limits, as well as an additional strip of land on the eastern side, forming a new township to be called Keene in honor of the governor's friend, Sir Benjamin Keene, who was at that time minister from England to Spain.

As the town grew, the need for stores to support the population grew with it. The EF Lane Hotel was originally built to be a general store. Goodnow's Department Store occupied the building for about one hundred years before closing in 1995, along with Woolworths and Sears. In 2001, after sitting idle for some time, the building was completely renovated, and the EF Lane Hotel was born.

Now functioning as a luxury boutique hotel, the EF Lane offers forty rooms, along with the Chase Tavern, which now serves lunch and dinner Tuesday through Saturday.

The 1995 movie *Jumanji* was filmed in Keene. Robin Williams came here in November 1994 for the shooting. Frank's Barber Shop is a featured setting, and those who have seen the movie will recognize the Parish Shoe sign, which had been painted for the film. It was removed and then repainted as a reminder for everyone of the time when Keene made the big screen.

EF Lane Hotel
30 Main Street
Keene, NH 03431
(603) 357-7070

Bacon Vinaigrette

Excellent tossed with fresh baby spinach

Sweat bacon and shallots in a medium saucepan and reserve fat.

Pour vinegar into a mixer. Add sugar, bacon, shallots, and fat from bacon.

Slowly whip in oil at high speed until incorporated.

YIELD

1 1/2 quarts

3 layers of New Hampshire
   applewood bacon, diced

2 shallots, minced

1/2 cup cider vinegar

1/3 cup sugar

2 cups 90/10 oil

1/4 pound unsalted butter

5 yellow onions, peeled and sliced

5 red onions, peeled and sliced

1 bunch leeks, cleaned and sliced

3 bulbs garlic, sliced

2 cups red wine

1 1/2 pints beef stock

1 quart fresh chicken stock

1 bunch scallions

2 tablespoons dried thyme

2 bay leaves

4 tablespoons fresh parsley, chopped

Salt and pepper to taste

Four Onion Soup

In a large saucepan, melt butter and sweat onions, leeks, and garlic until caramelized. Deglaze pan with red wine. Let wine come to a boil for 3 minutes, or until it reduces by half. Add beef and chicken stock and scallions, thyme, bay leaves, and parsley. Bring to a boil and then simmer for 20 minutes. Add salt and pepper to taste.

YIELD

Serves 8

Chocolate Pâté

Combine chocolate, wine, and cream in the top of a double boiler and melt over simmering water over low heat, stirring constantly, until mixture is smooth. Do not allow chocolate to get too warm. Remove from heat and whisk well.

Pour into 8" × 4" loaf pans lined with wax paper. Refrigerate overnight. Before serving, unmold and slice with a knife dipped in hot water.

SAUCE
Purée berries, sugar, and liquor (if used) in a blender until smooth.

PLATING
Make a pool of sauce on a plate. Slice pâté and place on the sauce.

YIELD
Serves 12

1 pound bittersweet chocolate, chopped

3/4 cup Syrah (or other red wine)

1/4 cup heavy whipping cream

SAUCE

2 pints fresh berries (raspberries, blackberries, strawberries, and/or blueberries)

1/2 cup sugar

1/4 cup Grand Marnier or blackberry liquor (optional)

THE MOUNT WASHINGTON HOTEL AND RESORT

Bretton Woods

Situated in scenic Bretton Woods is a masterpiece of Spanish Renaissance architecture. The Mount Washington Hotel was a two-year labor of love for hundreds of master craftsmen. This flamboyant marvel opened in 1902 and immediately became a summer haunt for poets, presidents, and princes.

Bretton Woods is part of a land grant made in 1772 by royal governor John Wentworth. The area was named after Bretton Hall, Wentworth's ancestral home in Yorkshire, England.

The Mount Washington Hotel was conceived and built by industrialist and New Hampshire native Joseph Stickney, who made his fortune in coal mining and the Pennsylvania Railroad. Ground was broken in 1900, and construction was completed in 1902 with the help of 250 Italian craftsmen. On July 28 of that year, the front doors of this grand hotel opened to the public.

The most luxurious hotel of its day, the Mount Washington catered to wealthy guests from Boston, New York, and Philadelphia. As many as fifty trains a day stopped at Bretton Woods's three railroad stations. One of these stations, Fabyan's, is now one of the resort's dining establishments.

The hotel has been host to countless celebrities, including Winston Churchill, Thomas Edison, Babe Ruth, and three U.S. presidents. In 1944, the Mount Washington hosted the Bretton Woods International Monetary Conference. Delegates from forty-four nations convened, establishing the World Bank and International Monetary Fund, setting the gold standard at $35 an ounce, and designating the U.S. dollar the backbone of international exchange. The signing of the formal documents took place in the Gold Room, located off the hotel lobby and now preserved as a historic site.

In 1978, the Mount Washington Hotel was listed in the National Register of Historic Places. In 1986, the hotel and the Bretton Arms Country Inn (also located on the property) were designated as National Historic Landmarks.

Today, this grande dame has been restored to her original grandeur. In 1991, a group of local entrepreneurs joined forces to preserve this historic property and ensure its place in the twenty-first century.

Situated in the heart of the White Mountain National Forest at the foot of Mount Washington, this two-thousand-acre private resort can accommodate groups of up to one thousand people year-round. Located on Route 302, just twenty minutes east of Interstate 93 and thirty minutes west of Route 16, the resort is easily accessible from all directions. A helicopter landing pad is available on resort grounds.

The Mount Washington Hotel and Resort is nestled in the Ammonoosuc River valley, ringed by the Presidential, Dartmouth, and Willey-Rosebrook ranges. Just three miles north of Crawford Notch, it offers breathtaking views dominated by Mount Washington, the highest peak in the Northeast. Mount Washington is famous for its unique alpine flora and a view described by P. T. Barnum as "the second greatest show on Earth." The area is noted for crisp, clean mountain air, spectacular scenery, and endless outdoor recreation.

The Mount Washington Hotel and Resort
Route 203
Bretton Woods, NH 03575
(603) 278-1000

Blue Cheese and Spiced-Walnut Terrine

NUTS

2 teaspoons salt

4 teaspoons cumin, ground

1 teaspoon cardamon, ground

1 teaspoon black pepper, ground

4 tablespoons olive oil

4 cups walnuts

3/4 cup sugar

TERRINE

4 pounds Maytag blue cheese, crumbled

10 ounces fresh chèvre

10 ounces cream cheese, room temperature

1 pound butter, room temperature

1/2 cup brandy

2 cups scallions, minced

1/2 cup parsley, minced

1/2 cup chives, minced

NUTS

Mix salt, cumin, cardamom, and pepper. Heat oil in a heavy skillet over medium heat. Add walnuts and sauté until light brown. Sprinkle sugar on nuts and sauté until sugar melts and turns light amber. Toss nuts with spices and cool.

TERRINE

Oil skinny terrine pan and line with plastic wrap. Combine 3 pounds of the blue cheese and the chèvre, cream cheese, and butter in a food processor and purée smooth. Transfer to a bowl and fold in brandy and scallions. Mix parsley and chives in a separate bowl. Pipe 1/3 of the cheese mix into the bottom of terrine mold and spread out evenly. Sprinkle this with 1/3 of the remaining crumbled blue cheese. Sprinkle 1/3 of the nuts over the crumbled cheese, then 1/3 of the parsley chive mix. Repeat until terrine mold is full.

Refrigerate overnight.

YIELD

Serves 16

Pan-Braised Hen with New Potatoes, Leeks, and Red Wine Sauce

BRAISED HENS

Combine chicken, mirepoix, bay leaves, peppercorns, parsley, salt, and wine. Mix well. Let sit overnight. Remove chicken from marinade. Strain and reserve liquid. Dust chicken with flour and brown in olive oil. Remove. Add reserved marinade liquid to the same pan and reduce by half. Add the chicken stock and the chickens and turn down to a simmer.

Cover with buttered parchment paper and finish in a 325-degree oven until tender but not falling apart.

Remove chicken from juice. Reduce juice and skim until it tastes good. Strain and beat in butter. Hold warm.

VEGETABLES

Heat up a little olive oil and throw in the pearl onions, mushrooms, pancetta, and leeks and allow to brown. Splash with a smidge of sauce. Hold warm.

PLATING

Place a bit of the smashed potatoes in the middle of the plate. Lay down some vegetables in front of the potatoes. Prop the chicken against the potatoes over the vegetables. Sauce around and sprinkle with thyme leaves and celery leaves. Serve it forth.

BRAISED HENS

8 Cornish game hens

2 1/2 pounds mirepoix, chopped fine

8 bay leaves, crushed

1 ounce black peppercorns, crushed

1 bunch parsley, rough chopped, stems and all

Kosher salt as needed

1 bottle red wine

Flour, as needed

Olive oil blend, as needed

1 gallon chicken stock

6 ounces butter

VEGETABLES

50 pearl onions

2 tablespoons olive oil

32 white mushrooms, quartered

4 ounces pancetta, diced medium

4 leeks, 2-inch bias-cut

4 pounds new potatoes, mashed using olive oil

Thyme leaves, as needed

Celery leaves, as needed

Note: Do not *hold chicken in the steam table; it will over-cook. Rewarm chicken to order in the sauce or hold warm above the stove.*

YIELD

Serves 16

Raspberry Soufflé

In a heavy pan over medium heat, mix the liqueur and raspberry purée. Bring to a boil. Combine the potato flour and water to make a slurry and stir into the purée mixture.

Cook and stir thoroughly until the mixture begins to thicken. This will happen very quickly. Chill.

Whip egg whites to soft peaks. Add sugar bit by bit until the whites are firm and glossy. Fold into the chilled berry purée mixture.

Butter a soufflé dish and sprinkle with sugar. Fill with mixture to the top and level off, removing excess. Bake in a 350-degree oven until well risen and slightly browned.

YIELD
Serves 6

7 ounces Chambord raspberry liqueur

1 pound, 2 ounces raspberry purée

2 7/8 ounces potato flour

7 ounces water

1 pound, 2 ounces egg whites

5 1/4 ounces sugar

Maine

BAR HARBOR INN
Bar Harbor

The late nineteenth century was a glorious time for the rich and famous. They traveled freely, often settling for short periods to visit with others of like persuasion and to maximize their enjoyment of the changing weather patterns along the eastern seaboard. Bar Harbor was a natural setting for many.

Enough people gathered here to prompt them to establish a social club on the island. With guests like the Vanderbilts, Pulitzers, and Morgans, the Oasis Club started in 1874 with the express purpose of promoting "literary and social culture." The club moved from rented quarters into its own building in 1887 and was then incorporated as the Mount Desert Reading Room.

The beautiful new cedar-shingled structure, designed by architect William Randolph Emerson, became the center of Bar Harbor social activities during the summers before World War I. President William Howard Taft was entertained there during his three-day stay in Bar Harbor in 1910. The club flourished for the next thirty-five years, and members saw their ranks swell with visiting yachtsmen whose lustrous boats lay moored in Frenchman Bay, as well as many officers of the U.S. Navy, whose ships made annual visits.

Ladies were not allowed in the club except by special arrangement until 1921. It was then that a restaurant was opened to the public, and the club, faced with ever-increasing maintenance costs, sought to attract more investors. By 1922, it was no longer feasible for the club to carry the financial burden, and it was sold to the Maine Central Railroad.

For the next twenty-five years, the building had several proprietors and served a variety of tenants. In 1933, a group of hotel owners organized the Shore Club to allow guests at local hotels the use of club facilities. During World War II, the U.S. Navy leased the building and utilized it as an observation headquarters.

The summer of 1947 saw rather unusual weather patterns in the area. Perhaps because of global warming, which had been progressing since the last ice age, the area fell victim to a lengthy draught. The fire began in the afternoon of October 17 in a cranberry bog. With a parched countryside devoid of rain, the fire burned for several days. More than seventeen thousand acres burned, and every hotel in Bar Harbor was destroyed. Damage exceeded $23 million in 1947 dollars. But the fires didn't just occur around Bar Harbor. Across the state, more than two hundred thousand acres and twelve hundred residences were destroyed in what was called "the year Maine burned."

In 1950, a group of townspeople joined together to develop the Hotel Bar Harbor with an initial forty-room wing. A twenty-room motel was added along the shore path in 1960. In 1987, the property was purchased by David J. Witham, who changed the name to the Bar Harbor Inn. By 1999 he had completely redeveloped the property. The inn now has 153 guest rooms with modern amenities and is considered by many to be one of Maine's finest oceanfront properties.

The Bar Harbor Inn is once again an oasis for both residents and tourists alike.

Bar Harbor Inn
Newport Drive
Bar Harbor, ME 04609
(207) 288-3351
(800) 248-3351

Roasted French Lamb Rack with Roasted Red Pepper Coulis

LAMB

2 seven-bone lamb racks

Olive oil for searing

2 tablespoons garlic, chopped

1 tablespoon rosemary

1 tablespoon herbs de Provence

1/4 cup whole-grain mustard

SAUCE

8 ounces roasted red peppers
(bottled)

2 tablespoons balsamic vinegar

3 tablespoons honey

1 1/2 teaspoons dry mustard

1/2 cup Dijon mustard

1 teaspoon dry crumbled
rosemary

LAMB

Sear French lamb racks in olive oil until brown on all sides. Combine garlic, rosemary, herbs de Provence, and whole-grain mustard and spread on top of lamb rack. Bake in oven at 350 degrees for about 30 minutes, or until desired temperature is reached. Remove from oven and let set several minutes before carving.

SAUCE

Combine sauce ingredients in a food processor and pulse until chopped and combined.

PRESENTATION

Pool the sauce on the plate and attractively display carved lamb rack. Garnish with fresh rosemary.

YIELD

Serves 2

Crepes Grand Marnier

CREPES

Reserve 4 crepes to prepare crepe basket. Sauté crepes in medium sauté pan in butter over moderate heat. When sautéing, sprinkle crepe with cinnamon sugar. When the crepe is golden brown, fold crepe in 1/4 sizes and remove to plate. For the crepe basket, sauté crepes in butter and cinnamon sugar, remove from pan, and let cool in a muffin pan or form basket over a bowl or cup.

SAUCE

Combine all ingredients in saucepan, heat over medium heat, and reduce slightly.

PRESENTATION

Place one crepe basket in the center of the plate and surround basket with 1/4 crepes. Fill basket with vanilla ice cream, top with sauce, and garnish with whipped cream and mint sprig. Use any remaining sauce to drizzle on crepes and garnish with fresh raspberries.

YIELD

Serves 4

CREPES

20 six-inch crepes or
     1 package fresh crepes

1/4 cup butter

1/4 cup cinnamon sugar

SAUCE

8 ounces orange marmalade

4 ounces orange juice or juice
     from 2 oranges

2 tablespoons honey

4 ounces Grand Marnier or
     Triple Sec

2 ounces butter

4 ounces dried apricots, chopped

PRESENTATION

4 large scoops French vanilla ice
     cream

Whipped cream as needed

Mint

Fresh raspberries

PASTRY CRUST

3 cups all-purpose flour

2 tablespoons cold shortening

1 teaspoon salt

1 tablespoon sugar

1/2 pound cold butter

1/2 cup ice water

FILLING

1 cup sugar

3 tablespoons all-purpose flour

2 tablespoons corn starch

6 cups frozen Maine blueberries

6 tablespoons butter

Zest of 1 lemon

TOPPING

Cinnamon

Sugar

Maine Blueberry Pie

PASTRY CRUST

In a mixing bowl, combine flour and shortening on low speed. Add salt and sugar. Slowly add pieces of cold butter to the mix. Combine until the butter pieces are the size of small peas.

Pour in very cold water all at once. Mix until the dough just forms a ball.

Divide dough into 2 equal pieces and roll out into circles approximately 10 inches in diameter. Place 1 circle into a 9-inch pie plate.

FILLING

Mix sugar, flour, and corn starch together. Toss with blueberries. Melt butter and pour over the blueberry mixture. Toss the filling together with the lemon zest.

Pour all filing into the prepared crust and top with remaining crust. Crimp edges of the crust together and cut a small hole in the top of the pie. Sprinkle with cinnamon and sugar.

Bake at 325 degrees for 1 hour, 15 minutes.

YIELD

Serves 7–8

BLACK POINT INN
Prouts Neck, Scarborough

Prouts Neck, Maine, was first colonized by English settlers in the 1600s. The area's rocky coast and dense pine forest made it appear dark from the water, inspiring the name Black Point. Discovered first by Native American Indians who came by canoe to fish the sea, Prouts Neck has long been an alluring destination.

Black Point's wealth of natural beauty and abundant wildlife attracted the Kahler family, who built the Black Point Inn in 1878. The colorful history of the Black Point includes rail barons, political leaders, and one of Maine's most famous native sons, world-renowned artist Winslow Homer. Originally known as Southgate House, the Black Point Inn was at one time just one of many grand hotels to call Prouts Neck home. Today, it is the area's sole remaining hotel and a landmark to gracious hospitality.

The Kahler family made an astute investment. Summer tourism led to a building boom for Prouts Neck in the late 1800s. The area was also a favorite of Winslow Homer, whose family owned a cottage just steps from the inn. This renowned painter spent twenty-five years here, painting and drawing inspiration from the sea surrounding the inn. His cottage still contains his studio, which is now open to the public on a limited basis during the summer.

In 1923, the inn was sold to the Sprague family, who increased its size and added guest cottages built especially for rail barons. Following Prohibition, the Black Point Inn's Oak Room became Prouts Neck's first speakeasy. During World War II, the Black Point Inn continued to thrive, while many other resorts were demolished, with some consumed by fire.

The Black Point Inn has changed ownership several times since the war; yet, an emphasis on Old World charm and tradition remains. In 1969, two gentlemen in short sleeves were asked to leave the cocktail lounge at 5:30 p.m. It did not matter that they were the governors of Connecticut and Rhode Island. The precedent had been set decades earlier.

 *216*

"For my part, I travel not to go anywhere, but to go.
I travel for travel's sake. The great affair is to move."

—Robert Louis Stevenson

Black Point Inn
510 Black Point Road
Prouts Neck, Scarborough, ME 04074
(207) 883-2500

Warm Parsnip Flan

This is a favorite at the inn, especially during the fall and winter. It is often served warm on a bed of greens as a first course or alongside braised lamb shank.

Preheat oven to 325 degrees.

Peel and cut the parsnips into 1-inch pieces. Place in a saucepan and cover with cold water. Bring to a boil and cook until tender when pierced with a fork (5–10 minutes). Drain and pat dry. Place in the work bowl of a food processor and purée. Add eggs one at a time. Add heavy cream, salt, and pepper and process briefly to mix. Add Parmesan. Butter 6 large ramekins and fill them with the mixture. Place ramekins in water bath and bake 35–40 minutes, until slightly puffed and an inserted knife comes out clean. Let rest 5–10 minutes and then turn out onto a bed of dressed organic baby greens.

YIELD

Serves 6

3 large parsnips

3 large eggs

1 cup heavy cream

1/4 teaspoon salt

1/8 teaspoon pepper

1 cup Parmesan cheese

2 tablespoons butter

6 cups organic baby greens

6 tablespoons unsalted butter

1 large onion, diced

9 celery stalks, diced

7 cups chicken stock

2 tablespoons flour

1 leek, finely julienned

1 medium carrot, peeled and
finely julienned

1 large celery stalk, finely
julienned

1 1/4 cups heavy cream

1/2 pound (2 cups) Stilton cheese,
crumbled

Salt and freshly ground white
pepper to taste

Cream of Celery and Stilton Soup

Here is an elegant soup served at the beginning of a multicourse dinner.

Melt 3 tablespoons butter in medium pot. Add onions and celery and cook over medium heat, partially covered until vegetables soften, about 10 minutes. Add stock and bring to a boil, cover, and simmer over medium-low heat for 30 minutes, or until vegetables are very tender. Purée in a food processor or blender and set aside.

Melt remaining 3 tablespoons of butter in the soup pot and add flour. Cook over low heat, stirring constantly for 1 minute. Gradually whisk in the celery purée. Bring to a boil and simmer until soup thickens slightly, about 10 minutes.

Remove dark green parts from the leek and cut in half lengthwise. Cut into 2-inch pieces and julienne lengthwise very thinly and rinse well.

Blanch the julienned leek, carrot, and celery in boiling water for 30 seconds and set aside.

Meanwhile purée the heavy cream, Stilton cheese, salt, and 1/4 teaspoon pepper in a food processor until smooth. Whisk into the soup. Add julienned vegetables and heat gently over low heat, being careful not to boil. Serve immediately in warm bowls.

YIELD

Serves 8

Beet and Celeriac Purée

This side dish is always an unexpected treat—a bright ruby-colored purée with a balancing flavor of that knobby, funny-looking root vegetable called celeriac.

Place butter in a saucepan over medium-low heat. Add onions then celeriac. Cover and let "sweat" until vegetables are soft, about 25 minutes. Add beets and cook another 20 minutes until completely heated through. Purée mixture in a food processor or blender until very smooth. Add salt and pepper to taste.

Serve immediately or reserve and reheat gently over medium-low heat, stirring occasionally, or microwave. Freezes very well.

YIELD

Serves 8

1/4 pound unsalted butter

1 1/2 cups onion, sliced

1 large celeriac, sliced

5 large beets, cooked, peeled, and cut into quarters

Salt and pepper to taste

THE COLONY HOTEL
Kennebunkport

In 1870 four gentlemen arrived by train in Kennebunkport, Maine, from Arlington, Massachusetts. They had come to purchase land on which to build a summer resort. During dinner in the small village of Saco nearby, the foursome discussed their plans. Enoch Cousens of Kennebunk overheard their conversation and suggested that they accompany him to the port. There they were shown several hundred acres of high ground along the Atlantic Ocean.

The men liked what they saw so much that they purchased seven hundred acres covering five miles of shore from Cape Porpoise to Lord's Point in Kennebunk. Samuel Damon, Richard Hodgen, Charles Goodwin, and John Townsend Trowbridge, together with a fifth investor, formed the Sea Shore Company and set about fulfilling their plans. Ironically, the sellers of the land thought it was worthless since its rocky shore offered no safe havens for fishing boats, and it could not be used for pastureland or farming.

In 1872, construction began on their grand summer resort, perched on a rock outcropping at the mouth of the Kennebunk River. The Ocean Bluff, the first hotel on Cape Arundel, opened for business on June 15, 1878, with 186 guests. Immediate success caused them to add a seventy-room addition in 1881. Over the next fifteen years, they added tennis courts, a dinning room for three hundred guests, electric lights, and another room addition.

January 30, 1898, brought disaster. On a bitterly cold winter night, the Ocean Bluff was destroyed by fire. When insurance would not cover the loss, the Sea Shore Company could not afford to rebuild. In 1904 a long section of the remaining structure was moved from the Ocean Bluff to become the Oceanic Hotel, which is now the Colony Hotel East House.

In 1905 it was reported that a syndicate would purchase the site of the burned Ocean Bluff and erect a large hotel. A new hotel was commissioned to be built in 1913 by R. W. Norton. This hotel was named the Breakwater Court and was built by George Clark, who also built the Old Fort Inn. In 1916, a contractor, Fred Towne, and a carpenter, George Emery, built a new addition.

The Breakwater Court was situated on the highest point of land in Kennebunkport, overlooking the ocean, the river, beaches, and the rocky coast. It accommodated up to 150 guests and ran successfully for many years. In June 1917, an addition was added to the hotel, increasing the capacity from 150 to 200 guests. This addition is the current north wing of the Colony Hotel.

A stay at the Breakwater Court would include your room and three meals a day. A carriage ride was extra. The current Colony Hotel Carriage House sits were the Breakwater's stables and carriage house were located. The Breakwater was sold to the Boughton family in 1948.

The Boughton family of Florida was new to the hotel business in Maine. George Boughton was a member of the Atlantic City swimming team, known as the Wonder Mermen, which had been national champions two years in a row. Swimming was his passion, and he brought the Blue Flames to Maine. This team of hotel employees would entertain guests at the pool with synchronized swimming displays. The Blue Flames performed every year until 2000.

The Boughton family changed the name of the Breakwater Court to the Colony Hotel and then proceeded to expand. In 1949 they acquired the beach across the street and then bought the East House in 1954. At the time, it was known as the Glen House and prior to that as the Oceanic. Redesigning their acquisition, they removed the top three of the East House's six floors.

To keep up with modern standards, the Boughtons began to make improvements. Horsehair mattresses and many of the old furnishings were discarded in the first few years of their ownership. Old fixtures, such as tubs on legs, were sold in the lobby. Old phones, boxed in oak, were replaced.

Although many improvements have been made over the years to update the hotel, it still retains its original charm and ambiance. Many of the original bed headboards, bureaus, and needlepoint rugs are still part of the décor of many rooms. The Colony Hotel is still owned by the Boughton family.

The Colony Hotel
140 Ocean Avenue
Kennebunkport, ME 04046
(207) 967-4374
(800) 552-2363

1/4 cup sugar

1 tablespoon dry mustard

1 teaspoon salt

1 large onion, minced

3 cups canola oil

1 cup cider vinegar

1 tablespoon celery seed

The Colony Hotel House Dressing

Mix sugar, dry mustard, salt, and onion. Very slowly add oil and vinegar. After all the oil and vinegar have been added, then add the celery seed.

YIELD

5 cups

Spicy Lobster Markland

Heat saucepan to medium high. Pour in oil and add shallots and garlic.

Add asparagus, stirring until hot. Add crushed red pepper, lobster, mustard, and cream. Add feta and salt and pepper to taste.

Add Parmesan and brown under the broiler.

Serve immediately over fettuccine.

✦ YIELD ✦

Serves 2

2 one-and-one-quarter-pound lobsters, cooked, shelled, and cut into 1-inch pieces

1 tablespoon olive oil

1/2 cloves shallots, chopped

1 clove of garlic, chopped

1 cup fresh asparagus, cut into 1-inch pieces

Crushed red pepper to taste

2 tablespoons Stonewall Kitchen raspberry mustard

1 cup heavy cream

2 tablespoons feta cheese

Salt and pepper to taste

2 tablespoons fresh Parmesan, grated

2 cups cooked fettuccine

1 quart frozen strawberries

1/2 cup water

1/2 cup orange juice

2 cups nonfat yogurt

2 cups low-fat sour cream

1/2 cup sugar

2 pints fresh strawberries

Strawberry Soup

Use either a blender or a handheld bur mixer to grind the strawberries. Add all the ingredients. You may want to add some half-and-half to make the soup creamy.

YIELD

Serves 10–12

THE PORTLAND REGENCY HOTEL & SPA

Portland

The Portland Regency Hotel & Spa owes its existence, as well as its prime location by Portland's working waterfront, to Cuba. Back in the late nineteenth century, the people of Cuba wanted independence from Spain. Following the United States' lead, they had already freed their slaves, and Cubans in general were more interested in commerce with their northern neighbor than with the Spanish government.

As the riots and insurrection spread across the island, many people in the United States became concerned that they had to do something to help. Portland's civic leaders were alarmed over the brewing trouble in Cuba and wished to ensure that their local militia was adequately trained. Mayor James P. Baxter declared, "The possession of quarters in a prominent place, where the men would always be under the public eye, would be the means of improving the morale of the force."

In 1895, a neoclassic armory was built at a cost of $20,000 for Maine's national guard. At the time it was regarded as one of the finest and best-equipped armories in New England.

The Cuban war of independence ended after Teddy Roosevelt formed a group known as the Rough Riders (see *Recipes from Historic Texas* and the Menger Hotel), who charged up San Juan Hill, defeating the defending Spanish forces and forcing Spain to sue for peace.

In addition to its use as an armory, the building's large drill hall also frequently served as a civic auditorium: at the turn of the twentieth century, the annual concerts of the Maine Music Festival were held in the building.

The State of Maine Armory, as it was known, was vacated by the Maine National Guard in 1941 when its troops came under federal control. At one point a caretaker was the lone occupant of the building, until city officials opened the armory to house the many soldiers, sailors, and marines who were temporarily stranded in Portland.

The U.S. Navy took control of the armory in 1942 and used it as a recreation center for the remainder of World War II. Following the war, the building once again served multiple purposes as a home to the national guard's citizen soldiers, a civic auditorium, and the city's public bath house.

This once outstanding facility was now eclipsed by more modern structures in town. The armory was nearly razed in 1962 when it was once again abandoned as surplus property by the national guard and taken over by the city of Portland. Many civic leaders now wanted to demolish the site and use it for waterfront parking.

Many veterans who had trained there opposed this "improvement plan." After a year of controversy, the State of Maine Armory was sold for $28,000 to State Paper Company. The building, which had served both Maine and the nation for over sixty years, was used as a warehouse until 1984, when it was purchased for conversion into a hotel.

The Portland Regency Hotel opened with ninety-five rooms in 1987, a complement to Portland's popular, restored Old Port. The exterior of the armory was preserved intact, with the exception of the skylight windows on the upper floors. Many of the original architectural elements create unique features in some of the spacious, traditionally appointed rooms. Highly detailed fireplaces, turreted corners, and windows of many shapes and sizes offer a special ambiance.

In 1990, the Portland Regency joined the National Trust for Historic Preservation as a distinguished member of the Historic Hotels of America. In August 2003 the Portland Regency Hotel became the Portland Regency Hotel & Spa following renovations and the addition of a fitness center and full day spa.

"The discovery of a new dish does more for the happiness of mankind than the discovery of a new star."

—A. Brillat-Savarin

The Portland Regency Hotel & Spa
20 Milk Street
Portland, ME 04101
(207) 774-4200
(800) 727-3436

Coriander Scallops with Apricot Sauce

Evenly coat each scallop with ground coriander and sauté in a hot pan with butter. Cook until browned on both sides and opaque in the center. Serve in a pool of apricot sauce. Sprinkle with basil leaves.

APRICOT SAUCE

Sweat the ginger root and shallot in a saucepan. Add the white wine and sun-dried apricots. Reduce the wine by half of its original volume. Add apricot preserves, browning sauce, salt, and white pepper. Bring to a boil for 5 minutes, or until sauce thickens.

Chef's note: Buy the freshest and largest scallops you can. Ask your fishmonger for "dry scallops." Plan on 6–8 ounces per person. Remember, the higher the count number on the scallops, the smaller they will be. Example: U30 count means there are approximately 30 scallops per pound and U10 means there are approximately 10 scallops per pound.

YIELD

Serves 6

---

3 pounds fresh, dry sea scallops

3/4 cup ground coriander

2 tablespoons butter

APRICOT SAUCE

2 teaspoons ginger root, minced

1 teaspoon shallot, minced

1 cup white wine (Chablis)

20 sun-dried apricots, finely diced

2 cups apricot preserves

1/2 teaspoon browning sauce

1/4 teaspoon salt

1/4 teaspoon white pepper

4 eight-ounce portions of fresh Atlantic salmon fillets

CITRUS MAYONNAISE

Zest of 1/2 lemon, lime, and orange

Juice of 1 lime

1 cup mayonnaise

Pinch of salt and pepper

PISTACHIO TOPPING

1 cup pistachio meats, coarsely ground

1/2 cup plain bread crumbs

4 tablespoons butter, melted

ORANGE-FENNEL RELISH

1 fennel bulb

1/2 red onion

1 cup orange juice

1 cup orange marmalade

1 1/2 teaspoons ground coriander

1 1/2 teaspoons ginger root, minced

Salt and pepper to taste

Pistachio-Encrusted Salmon with Orange-Fennel Relish

CITRUS MAYONNAISE

Mix all of the ingredients together and set aside in refrigerator.

PISTACHIO TOPPING

Mix all of the ingredients together until moist.

ORANGE-FENNEL RELISH

Julienne the fennel and red onion, then caramelize in a sauté pan.

Add the orange juice and reduce until 1/2 of the original volume is gone.

Add marmalade and cook until mixture starts to thicken.

Stir in coriander, ginger root, salt, and pepper.

Remove from heat and allow to cool to room temperature while preparing and cooking salmon.

FINAL PREPARATION

Place salmon fillets in a well-greased baking dish (skin side down).

Spread mayonnaise over the tops of the salmon fillets.

Sprinkle pistachio mixture over mayonnaise (press into mayonnaise slightly).

Bake salmon at 350 degrees for approximately 20 minutes, or until sides feel firm.

Serve each portion with a side of the orange-fennel relish.

~❧ YIELD ❧~

Serves 4

1 cup extra virgin olive oil

2 tablespoons garlic, minced

Zest and juice of 1 lemon

1/2 teaspoon red chili flakes

1 1/2 teaspoons rosemary leaves,
    rough chopped

1 1/2 teaspoons savory leaves,
    rough chopped

1 teaspoon salt

1/2 teaspoon cracked black
    pepper

1 quart of your favorite olives
    (4 or 5 varieties is nice)

Marinated Olives

Whisk all the ingredients together and toss with your olives.

The olives will keep for a couple of weeks in the refrigerator, but should be served at room temperature.

❧ YIELD ❧

Serves 12

THE WHITE BARN INN

Kennebunkport

The attraction of the Kennebunkport region was well recognized by Native Americans, who hunted game in the forests and fished the local waters. In the early 1600s, French and English explorers established trading posts and fishing camps, lured by the success of the Indian population. The white pine and hardwood forests spawned a shipbuilding and shipping community that flourished for the next 250 years. Trading encompassed the entire eastern seaboard of North America, as well as the West Indies, Europe, and the Far East.

Toward the end of the nineteenth century, as shipbuilding and shipping activities declined in importance, the area started benefiting from a new force: resort living. Modern conveniences in bustling cities encouraged many wealthier people to escape to the countryside or shore to reconnect with nature.

In 1820 the Forest Hill House was built to accommodate the influx of vacationers. It would eventually be called the White Barn Inn, drawing its name from the ever-present storage facility on the property. Constructed in a typical New England style, the house with its outlying property was purchased in the late 1800s by the Boothby family, who transformed it into an inn catering mainly to a Jewish clientele. They divided the upper floors into guest rooms and added a wraparound porch with Victorian details. The ground floor became spacious living and dining rooms.

When the railroad built a new route and station at Kennebunkport in 1872, Bostonians could suddenly reach the area with a three-hour train ride. Business boomed as word of mouth and press reports proclaimed the excellent dining available at this extraordinary inn.

Today, the common rooms of the White Barn Inn retain their old-fashioned appeal, with nineteenth-century-style upholstery and wallpapers, antique portraits, and oriental carpets laid on hardwood floors. The main floor of the barn has been transformed into a dinning room that marries rustic architecture with elegant accoutrements. Both the rooms in the old house and the more recently constructed cottagelike suites capture the charm of the original inn, which blends easily into the woods that surround the hilltop property.

The restaurant has a varied menu greatly influenced by local ingredients. Game dishes such as guinea hens, turkey, and venison are often garnished with wild mushrooms, New England cranberries, and preserved Maine blueberries gathered in the area by local foragers. Lobster, cod, and shrimp dishes are regular seaside favorites.

The White Barn Inn
37 Beach Avenue
Kennebunk, ME 04043
(207) 967-2321

Pesto

Properly stored, pesto will keep without changing color for several days. Transfer the finished pesto to a nonreactive glass or stainless steel container. Pour a thin layer of olive oil over the pesto and cover the container with aluminum foil to keep out light and air.

Combine the basil, parsley, garlic, cheese, and olive oil in the bowl of a food processor and pulse until finely chopped. Add the pistachios, pine nuts, and walnuts and chop for a few more seconds, being careful not to overprocess the mixture. The nuts should be chopped to a medium texture but not finely ground. Season the pesto with salt and pepper to taste. Refrigerate until ready to use.

YIELD
1 1/2 cups

1 bunch fresh basil leaves

1/2 bunch fresh flat-leaf parsley

1 clove garlic

3/4 cup Parmesan cheese, freshly grated

1 cup olive oil

1/4 cup pistachios, shelled

1/4 cup pine nuts

1/4 cup walnuts, shelled

Salt and freshly ground pepper

2 pounds watermelon, peeled, seeded, and cut into chunks

1 pound bing cherries, pitted

1 cup white dessert wine, such as Muscat

1 cup chilled champagne

Iced Watermelon and Bing Cherry Soup

The trick to making chilled fruit soups is to keep them light and well balanced in flavor. A soup that's too sweet will overwhelm the palate. The addition of champagne adds an effervescent note. Be sure to serve this as soon as you stir in the chilled champagne.

In a food processor, purée the watermelon, cherries, and white wine until smooth. Strain through a fine sieve into a serving bowl or pitcher, cover, and refrigerate. Just before serving, stir in the chilled champagne.

YIELD

Serves 4

Strawberry Jam

Nothing will make afternoon tea guests feel more special than a bowl filled with just-made jam. This strawberry preserve is easy to make and can be eaten as soon as it cools. Any remaining jam may be canned in glass jars, following proper canning procedures, and stored for up to six months.

In a large, heavy-bottomed saucepan, combine the strawberries, sugar, and lemon juice. Bring to a boil over medium-high heat. Reduce the heat to medium low and simmer uncovered for 30 minutes, stirring occasionally, until the mixture is reduced by half. Cool and serve, or can in glass jars according to proper canning techniques.

❧ YIELD ❧
1 quart

4 cups ripe strawberries, rinsed, cored, and quartered

3 cups sugar

Juice of 1 lemon

Connecticut

ALTNAVEIGH INN AND RESTAURANT

Storrs

Early Connecticut pioneer and settler John Sargeant purchased 120 acres of land on Spring Hill from Thomas Huntington in 1716. Not only was Sargeant one of the principle members of the local church, having signed the covenant, but he was also considered to be one of the leading citizens of Mansfield, known then as Pond Place. Mansfield sits astride what is today called the Boston Turnpike, or state route 44.

Spring Hill was an attractive site, and Sargeant's son, Isaac, elected to stay there upon his marriage. John gave his son part of the land, and he built a home there. An attic beam records a date of 1734, which is assumed to be the original date of the construction of the house.

Isaac and his wife, Ann, lived there for many years, acquiring most of the original 120 acres from his father when he died. Upon Ann's death in 1794, the house and eighty-nine acres were sold to Dan Storrs. The town is named after Dan's family, but he eventually decided to sell the house to Azariah Freeman. The Freeman family maintained the house for the next 113 years, and noted nineteenth-century miniaturist George Freeman is believed to have occupied this house for a period.

The house was purchased by Edith McComb in 1951 and used as an inn and restaurant. She was quite fond of Gaelic culture and named the house Altnaveigh, which means "hill top." Located near the present day University of Connecticut along Route 195, the Spring Hill area and Altnaveigh offer charm, elegant dining, and quaint lodging in a restored 1730s home.

Altnaveigh was purchased by its present owners, Douglas and Gail Parks, in 2004. They immediately undertook an ambitious renovation to restore the house to its original grandeur and modernize the kitchen facilities.

> *"One cannot think well, love well, and sleep well, if one has not dined well."*
>
> —Virginia Woolf

Altnaveigh Inn and Restaurant
957 Storrs Road (Route 195)
Storrs, CT 06268
(860) 429-4490

Oyster Stew

Staked by many to be the world's best!

Melt butter in a heavy skillet over medium heat. Add onions and cook until tender. Add potatoes and carrots and sauté mixture for 1 minute. Add half-and-half and heavy cream to mixture and turn heat to high. As mixture approaches a boil, turn heat back down to medium and add oysters and their liquid. Season stew with salt and pepper to taste. Cook until oysters curl at edges. Finish with a pinch of cayenne. Serve in warm bowls with garlic toast points.

YIELD

Serves 4

1 tablespoon butter

1 small onion (white or yellow), diced

1 cup potatoes, diced and cooked

1 cup carrots, diced and cooked

2 cups half-and-half

2 cups heavy cream

2 twelve-ounce containers of fresh shucked oysters (with liquid)

Salt and fresh cracked black pepper to taste

Pinch of cayenne pepper

Garlic toast points

POPOVERS

6 medium eggs

1 cup flour

1 tablespoon sugar

1 tablespoon butter

Pinch of kosher salt

Pinch of cracked pepper

1 cup whole milk

2 tablespoons butter, melted

MAPLE BUTTER

1 stick butter

1/4 cup maple syrup

Not Just Any Popovers!

POPOVERS

Preheat oven and muffin pan to 400 degrees. In large bowl, beat eggs until smooth. Add flour, sugar, butter, salt, pepper, and milk. Beat until batter is smooth.

Remove hot muffin pan from oven. Spray or grease with vegetable oil. Ladle batter into muffin tins until half way up the side of each. Place in oven and cook until golden brown and puffy (approximately 30 minutes). Serve piping hot with whipped butter or maple butter recipe.

MAPLE BUTTER

Whip butter and maple syrup with electric beater until creamy and twice its volume. Serve in ramekins with popovers.

YIELD

Serves approximately 12

New England
Butter Pound Cake

Preheat oven to 350 degrees. Grease and flour a bundt pan and put aside. Cream butter and sugar until sugar is somewhat dissolved. Add eggs one at a time until well blended and then stir in the milk. Combine flour, baking powder, and salt and sift in a quarter at a time. Finish by adding the vanilla and the butter flavoring. Pour into prepared bundt pan and cook at 350 degrees for 1 hour, or until toothpick comes out clean. When cool, dust with confectioners' sugar and serve with berries and cream.

YIELD

1 Bundt cake

3 sticks butter

3 cups sugar

6 whole eggs

1 cup whole milk

3 cups flour

1 teaspoon baking powder

1/4 teaspoon salt

1 teaspoon vanilla extract

2 tablespoons real butter flavoring

Confectioners sugar

Berries

Cream

THE INN AT WOODSTOCK HILL

Woodstock

John Truesdell built the main house of the inn back in 1816 for William Bowen. William was a descendant of Henry Bowen, one of the thirteen "Goers" who settled Woodstock in 1686. He was also a selectman of Woodstock, a founder of Woodstock Academy, the proprietor of the Asa Bishop Tavern, and the town's first postmaster.

Plaine Hill, as the main house is known, is situated prominently at the southern approach to Woodstock Hill. Plaine Hill has undergone a number of reconstructions, renovations, and additions over the years. As it appears today, the massive clapboard house has a steeply pitched hip roof and dormers on all faces. The main entrance is marked by a segmental pediment, which, because of an addition to the northern façade, is asymmetrically placed.

A large attached barn, which had extended to the south of the main house, recently collapsed and was removed; it may be rebuilt in the future. A small cottage is on the property to the south of the main house. Built in 1900 and renovated in 1987, this structure has a center chimney, two small dormers on the front, and a shed dormer across the full length of the back.

Following the death of William Bowen, the property passed to his son, Col. Matthew Bowen, and then to his son, Andrew Williams Bowen, who sold it to his cousin, Henry C. Bowen. Henry Bowen built nearby Roseland Cottage.

The Bowen family connection continued through Henry C. Bowen's son, Herbert W. Bowen, who served as a diplomat, then retired to Woodstock in the early part of the twentieth century. He passed the property on to Gardner Richardson, his nephew. The property remained in the Bowen family until after the death of Gardner Richardson's widow, Dorothea. She bequeathed the farm to the University of Connecticut in 1981 as a memorial to their son, Lt. Peter Bowen Richardson, USAF, who was killed during the Korean War.

The farm was returned to the family in 1985, and the buildings and adjacent land were subsequently sold to a group of investors who converted the main house and barn into an inn and restaurant, known today as the Inn at Woodstock Hill. The majority of the farmland remains in the Bowen family, just as it has for three centuries.

The Inn at Woodstock Hill's restaurant has been featured in *Connecticut Magazine*, which awarded it "Best Hotel Dining" and "Best Brunch." In addition, the inn and restaurant have been featured in numerous publications, including *Country Inns*, *People*, *Country Inns and Backroads*, *Yankee Magazine*, *Yankee Traveler*, and *Worcester Magazine*. It is also listed on the National Register of Historic Places.

The Inn at Woodstock Hill
94 Plaine Hill Road
Woodstock, CT 06281-2912
(860) 928-0528

Venison Stew

1/2 cup vegetable oil

Flour to coat venison

1 pound venison, cut into 1/2-inch cubes

1/2 cup onion, diced

4 garlic cloves, minced

3 bay leaves

1/2 cup celery, diced

1/2 cup carrots, diced

3 cups beef or venison stock

2 cups apple cider

3 small red potatoes, chopped

1/2 cup red pepper

1/4 cup green pepper, diced

1/4 cup yellow pepper, diced

1/2 cup fresh fennel (anise), chopped

3 tablespoons balsamic vinegar

3 tablespoons herbs de Provence (substitute 1 tablespoon rosemary, 1 tablespoon thyme, 1 tablespoon oregano)

1/2 cup porcini mushrooms

2 tablespoons Worcestershire sauce

Tabasco and salt to taste

Scallions, sliced finely, and cracked black pepper for topping

Heat a pot with 1/2 cup of vegetable oil at the highest setting. Toss the venison in flour and carefully place in the pot when the oil is good and hot. Stir venison until it's browned on all sides and then put in the onions. Continue stirring for another 2 minutes. Turn the heat down to medium-high and add the garlic and bay leaves. Stir for another minute and add the celery, carrots, stock, and cider. Bring the mixture to a boil and then simmer for 10 minutes. Add the potatoes and simmer for another 10 minutes. Add the red, green, and yellow peppers, fennel, vinegar, herbs, mushrooms, and Worcestershire sauce. Cook for 5 more minutes, or until potatoes are tender. Turn off the heat, remove the bay leaves, and season to taste.

For a thicker stew, add a small amount of beurre manié (mixture of flour and soft butter) to the stew during its final simmer.

SOME NICE VARIATIONS

Substitute 1 tablespoon of curry powder for the balsamic vinegar.

Add 2 tablespoons finely chopped chipotle peppers (smoked jalapeño peppers available dried or canned in most gourmet markets).

Add 1 cup of chorizo sausage and substitute 2 table-spoons paprika for the herbs de Provence.

⤖ YIELD ⥿

Serves 4–6

2 cups milk

2 cups heavy cream

3 whole eggs

7 egg yolks

1 cup sugar

2 teaspoons vanilla extract

Pinch of salt

1/2 cup Amaretto or other liquor

Fresh fruit

Whipped cream

Amaretto Crème Brûlée

A cool creamy dessert on a warm summer evening

Preheat the oven to 310 degrees. Put the milk and cream in a saucepan to warm over a low heat. Whip the whole eggs and yolks and slowly add the hot liquid while whisking. Mix in the sugar, vanilla, salt, and Amaretto (Tia Maria, schnapps, and flavored brandies also work well). Place ramekins or other thick, shallow porcelain dishes into a roasting pan and fill the pan with enough water to reach halfway up the dishes. Then pour the brûlée mixture into the ramekins. Carefully place in the oven and bake for at least 20 minutes; baking may take as long as 30 minutes. When the crème brûlée is firm and slightly brown on top, remove it from the oven and place it in the refrigerator to cool.

Finish the crème brûlée by spreading a thin layer of sugar over the top and caramelize (melt and brown the sugar) with a torch. They sell special (small and expensive) torches, but a simple propane torch from the hardware store will do the trick. Be sure to caramelize the crème brûlée over a nonflammable surface; an inverted sheet pan works well. Wait a minute to allow the sugar to cool and then garnish with fresh fruit and whipped cream!

YIELD

Serves 6–8

Apple Butternut Squash Soup

Bring the broth to a boil in a large stock pot. Drop the sliced apples in and allow them to poach for 5 minutes. Take off the heat. Combine squash, sugar, cardamom, nutmeg, and garam masala in the pot and stir thoroughly. Purée the ingredients in batches in a good processor at the highest speed. Only add the half-and-half if the soup will be eaten immediately; otherwise, add the half-and-half to the soup just before you reheat it. The soup (without the half-and-half) will keep in the refrigerator for up to a week. Serve topped with toasted coconut or toasted pumpkin seeds.

Garam masala is an Indian spice blend that can be found in most good gourmet or natural food stores. If you can't find any, you can substitute a good-quality curry powder (1/2 to 1 teaspoon). Although the flavor won't be exactly the same, it will still be good!

YIELD

Serves 10

4 cups vegetable broth (chicken broth may be substituted)

1 Granny Smith apple, sliced

3 cups butternut squash, cooked

1/3 cup brown sugar

1/3 teaspoon ground cardamom

1/2 teaspoon ground nutmeg

1/2 teaspoon garam masala*

1 cup half-and-half

Toasted coconut or pumpkin seeds to garnish

THE INTERLAKEN RESORT & CONFERENCE CENTER

Lakeville

The Interlaken Inn, originally a modest farmhouse, was erected around 1760. The site became a prime spot for an inn as it sat astride the stagecoach trail that connected Hartford, Connecticut, with Poughkeepsie, New York, and the Hudson River. During the eighteenth century, the inn was believed to be a regular stop for weary stagecoach travelers passing through the Taconic Range (western New York and eastern Connecticut).

During the early part of the nineteenth century, vast amounts of raw iron products produced in Lakeville and Salisbury, Connecticut, were transported over this same overland route to the Hudson River for delivery to customers up and down the eastern seaboard. Due to the quality of Salisbury iron ore, iron producers and foundries in the area provided 80 percent of the cannons used by George Washington's army during the Revolutionary War.

The Shaw family purchased this farm property in 1891 and erected the inn, plus four houses adjacent to it, to take advantage of all the people passing through. Only one of these houses remains part of the inn's property: Sunnyside, a restored Victorian-period structure with multiple guest rooms and fireplaces and a wide wraparound porch. The other three dwellings have evolved into neighboring homes.

The Shaws operated the Interlaken Inn for thirty-four years until they sold it to John and Elizabeth Percy in 1924. At this time, the inn still lacked modern conveniences. They modernized the inn by installing electricity throughout to replace acetylene gas lights, a heating plant, running water, and a bath for each guest room. The Interlaken Inn became quite a modern marvel for that era.

The Percys decided to retire in 1956 after operating the inn for over thirty years. They sold the property to Anthony Peters, who made considerable modernizing improvements. The restoration program was near completion in the spring of 1971 when a catastrophic blaze totally destroyed the inn on May 20, the week before its planned weekend opening.

The rebuilt Interlaken Inn was officially opened in October 1973 and has since gained a prominent reputation as a quality New England inn in a resortlike setting between two picturesque lakes.

In May 1982, Paul and Steven Reisman purchased the Interlaken Inn and immediately began to expand the services and facilities to provide a conference center, while maintaining the inn's countrylike atmosphere.

Today, the Interlaken Inn comprises thirty acres in the foothills of the Berkshires, near the wooded shores of Connecticut's Lake Wononscopomuc. Guests can swim, boat, or fish in a lake that is so crystal clear one can see straight to the bottom in twenty feet of water. The inn supplies rowboats, kayaks, and canoes. Other recreational amenities include two all-weather tennis courts, an outdoor heated swimming pool, a basketball court, volleyball, and the Executive Hospitality Center, which includes a large-screen TV, a pool table, and a fully furnished exercise room. Massage services are also available in this building.

The Interlaken Resort & Conference Center
74 Interlaken Road
Route 112
Lakeville, CT 06039
(860) 435-9878
(800) 222-2909

2 pounds scallops

SPRING PEA PURÉE

2 cups sweet peas, shucked

1/4 cup cream

Salt to taste

Pinch of sugar if needed

FAVA BEAN AND LEMON
RELISH

1 cup fava beans, shucked

1/8 cup extra virgin olive oil

Salt and pepper

Pinch of tarragon, chopped

Zest and juice of 2 lemons

Sea Scallops with Spring Pea Purée and Fava Bean and Lemon Relish

One of the Interlaken's most-asked-for recipes! Fresh flavors, light in composition, and so delicious, this recipe can be prepared from ingredients found in most kitchens.

SPRING PEA PURÉE

Boil shucked peas in salted water for 3 minutes. Strain and reserve liquid. Purée peas with 1 cup of cooking liquid in a blender until smooth. Add cream to smooth out purée. Season with salt and sugar if needed.

FAVA BEAN AND LEMON RELISH

Place boiled and shucked spring fava beans in a mixing bowl. Add extra virgin olive oil, salt, pepper, and a pinch of chopped tarragon and grated lemon zest with lemon juice to taste. Mix and set aside.

SCALLOPS

Sear sea scallops in a hot skillet until crispy and brown on both sides. They should be slightly underdone in center.

YIELD

Serves 8

Local Sweet Corn Soup

A seasonal favorite that will change the way you think about corn soup! Using fresh corn from farmer Bill Johnson (just down the road from the Interlaken), the chef chose sweet "butter-and-sugar" corn for this recipe and only purchased corn that was picked that day.

CORN STOCK

Cut corn kernels off the cob. Reserve corn kernels for soup. Place cobs with one sliced onion in a stockpot and cover with cold water. Cook for 1 1/2 hours. Strain.

CORN SOUP

Sautee 2 sliced onions in butter until translucent. Add corn kernels and cook for 2 minutes. Add 6 cups of corn stock. Cook soup base for about 5 minutes.

Purée in blender until very smooth. Return to stove in a new saucepan. Bring to boil and finish with cream. Add salt to taste. Serve.

⟞ YIELD ⟝

Serves 10–12

30 ears of corn

3 onions, sliced

1/4 pound butter

1 cup heavy cream

Salt

3 shots of vodka

2 shots of blood orange purée

1/2 shot of Triple Sec

Champagne

Blood orange, sliced into wedges,
   for garnish

Morgan's Blood Orange Champagne Cocktail

The signature cocktail for Morgan's Restaurant at Interlaken Inn, this concoction offers flavor, color, and quite a kick.

In a pint glass filled with ice, add vodka, blood orange purée, Triple Sec, and champagne. Shake well and serve in a chilled martini glass with a blood orange wedge.

✺ YIELD ✺

Serves 1

LIGHTHOUSE INN RESORT
New London

Steel magnate Charles S. Guthrie built the Lighthouse Inn Resort in 1902. Originally called Meadow Court because of the wildflowers that surrounded it, the mansion was Guthrie's grand summer home on the waterfront. Designed by noted architect William Emerson of Boston, the home commanded a breathtaking view of Long Island Sound.

The mansion's formal grounds were conceived by renowned landscape architect Frederick Law Olmsted, the noted designer who created New York City's Central Park. Meadow Court quickly became a popular venue for regal social events and a private retreat for Guthrie's rich and famous friends, including film stars like Bette Davis and Joan Crawford.

After Guthrie's untimely death in 1906, Meadow Court served many years as a private residence until it was sold by his widow in 1925. The new owners began operating the mansion as an inn in 1927. It was then renamed the Lighthouse Inn Resort after the nearby New London Harbor Light.

In September 1912, *American Homes and Gardens* magazine said, "There are few homes in America more attractively situated than the property of Mrs. Charles S. Guthrie, in New London, CT. This is the embodiment of the ideas of what a house should be."

The inn became a National Historic Landmark in 1996. Today, the Lighthouse Inn Resort is a member of the Prestigious Historic Hotels of America. It has achieved this status because it exemplifies what an elegant property on Connecticut's beautiful waterfront should be.

Lighthouse Inn Resort
6 Guthrie Place
New London, CT 06320
(860) 443-8411
(888) 443-8411

Stolichnaya vodka

Half-and-half cream

Freshly ground nutmeg

Walkup's Russian Quaalude Martini

This is a great after-dinner martini—refreshing, light, and very settling. However, beware! This is a very sneaky cocktail! You will not know what hit you until it is too late! Just like good marketing. Cheers!

Fill martini glass with crushed ice and water. Leave to chill.

Fill cocktail shaker with ice and approximately 4 ounces of vodka.

Add approximately 2 ounces half-and-half to shaker. Shake contents repeatedly until ice coating forms on cocktail shaker. Contents should resemble frothy milk.

Empty chilling martini glass and strain Russian Quaalude into chilled martini glass.

Sprinkle ground nutmeg on top of cocktail *very lightly* . . . a very light dusting!!

Sit back and feel the effects of Walkup's Russian Quaalude martini!

Do not operate any machinery!

YIELD

Serves 1

Timothy's Famous Lobster Crepes

The secret recipe!!

Lobster mushroom Madeira-cream crepe appetizer. Very elegant and easy to make.

SAUCE

Add shallots, cream, Madeira, and mushrooms in a pan. Reduce until the sauce is thickened. Add lobster and fresh chives. Season with salt and pepper and wrap in a crepe.

Sprinkle the top of the crepe with a few fresh chives. Elegant and very delicious!

CREPES

In a large bowl, mix eggs, milk, and salt very well.

In an additional large bowl, add flour and slowly add in the beaten egg-milk-salt mixture. There must be no lumps.

Add melted butter by whisking into the mixture.

Use a "seasoned" 8-inch pan.

SAUCE

1/4 pound shallots

12 tablespoons cream, heavy (about 40 percent)

5 tablespoons wine (Madeira Waterbury)

1 ounce mushrooms (Cul Lar)

3 ounces lobster meat

1/8 ounce fresh chives

1/8 ounce salt (sea salt or kosher)

1/8 ounce white pepper, ground

CREPES

9 eggs, large and beaten

3 cups milk

1/8 ounce salt

2 cups all-purpose flour

12 ounce unsalted butter

HOW TO "SEASON" A PAN

Place crepe pan on high heat and add 3 tablespoons of salt and 1/4 cup of oil. Leave pan on high heat until oil begins to smoke. Drain the oil and, using a cotton cloth, work salt around until the whole pan has an oily glow.

❧ YIELD ❧

32 crepes

Chilled Seafood Pasta Salad

The chef's personal, supersecret chilled seafood salad recipe. Although is seems very simple and ordinary, the result is a very refreshing, filling, and delightful main course. The secrets to the flavor of this dish are twofold:

1. continually stirring/mixing the salad while it processes

2. preparing the salad two days in advance of serving.

The longer the salad is in the refrigerator (and the more it is stirred), the better the seafood flavor and the better the blending of the simple flavors.

Boil pasta in water that has been seasoned with sea salt. Drain and chill in refrigerator.

Individually flash-boil large and small scallops (4–5 minutes maximum for large scallops and 2–3 minutes for bay scallops. Immediately drain, pat dry, and place in refrigerator to chill.

Devein shrimp. Boil in sea-salted water until tender. If precooked, flash-boil 2–3 minutes, drain, pat dry, and place in refrigerator to chill.

Finely chop onions, celery hearts, and celery leaves and mix extremely well. Squeeze 4 large lemons into mixture and stir well. Refrigerate to chill.

Chop large sea scallops into quarter sections. Leave half of the small bay scallops whole and cut the rest in half.

3–4 pounds bowtie pasta (tricolor if possible)

Sea salt

2 pounds fresh large sea scallops

2 pounds Niantic bay scallops

2–3 pounds jumbo shrimp

2 sweet Vidalia onions, medium

1 package of celery hearts (use all healthy greenery from celery stalk as this adds nice flavor)

8 large lemons

3 large scoops (~2 cups) mayonnaise

Slice half of the shrimp directly down the middle; chop the other half up completely.

Blend all ingredients (except pasta) into large bowl. Mix well! Squeeze 2 more lemons into mixture. Mix well!

Add mayonnaise, salt and pepper to taste. Blend until creamy and well spread throughout seafood mixture.

Add chilled pasta and mix well again! Squeeze 2 more lemons into mixture. Continue to stir so that it is thoroughly blended.

Cover well. Chill for at least 1 day. Stir throughout each day. Add extra mayo if needed.

YIELD
Serves 20

THE SPA AT NORWICH INN

Norwich

The original Norwich Inn was built in 1929 and served as a haven for the rich and famous of the time. Charles Laughton, Frank Sinatra, George Bernard Shaw, and the Prince of Wales found time to spend here. Drawn by its architectural elegance and stunning surroundings, they found the inn a convenient stopping spot halfway between Boston and New York.

The Norwich Inn has graced these Connecticut woods for eighty years with its Georgian Colonial Revival structure and its handsome front portico, door, and fanlight. Despite its grand attraction for the rich and famous, it changed hands several times during the war years. Eventually, it entered a period of decline until it was ultimately purchased by the city of Norwich. The upstairs continued to support guests as a boardinghouse while the local police used the basement to house the overflow of prisoners from the Norwich jail. The original expansive, rolling-hills golf course continued to operate and today is a high-quality course open to the public.

In 1983, the Edward J. Safdie Group bought the property. Their objective was to remake this inn in the mold of California's Sonoma Mission Inn and Spa (see *Recipes from Historic California*). Mr. Safdie renovated the entire property to convert the original 75 guest rooms into 100, and he added 160 condominium villas on the 42 acres. He also built a freestanding spa facility that attracted such stars as Joan Rivers, Cheryl Tiegs, Barbra Streisand, Elle Macpherson, Rachel Hunter, and Michael Douglas.

Safdie's new style for the Norwich Inn and Spa was the epitome of glamour and beauty. It attracted the interest of the Mashantucket Pequot Tribal Nation, which purchased the property in 1994. Their $15 million renovation doubled the size of the spa, making it the largest spa on the East Coast when it was completed. All of the guest rooms and villas were also redecorated, and the project concluded with the renaming of the facility as the Spa at Norwich Inn.

The Spa at Norwich Inn is an intimate retreat and home to an elegant, full-service spa. It offers a blend of fitness programs, nutritional instruction, and beauty and body treatments designed to restore and rejuvenate guests. Management's focus is on personal attention. Guests do not have to conform to routines, regimens, or schedules. Rather, the spa's staff makes a point of conforming to

 *260*

the individual needs of guests, who may choose from a range of program packages or select from an à la carte menu of services and amenities.

The Spa at Norwich Inn continues to welcome the celebrities of the day, such as Hilary Swank and Chris Rock, along with another generation of the rich and famous, who come to be pampered, soothed, relaxed, and renewed in the privacy and peace of the Connecticut woods.

"The second day of a diet is always easier that the first. By the second day, you're off it."

—Jackie Gleason

The Spa at Norwich Inn
607 West Thames Street
Norwich, CT 06360
(800) 275-4772

Amaretto Shrimp Appetizer

SAUCE

Combine all the ingredients in a small bowl using a small wire whisk or spoon. Set aside, keeping at room temperature.

BLOSSOM SALAD

Gently toss blossoms and other ingredients with dressing.

SHRIMP

Toss the shrimp in the seasoned cornstarch until evenly coated; dust off any excess powder.

Heat a small skillet on medium-high and add the olive oil. Allow the olive oil to smoke lightly before adding the shrimp. Cook the shrimp until they spring back to the touch, about 2 minutes on each side. Do not overcook.

Place the cooked shrimp in a clean bowl and add the sauce. Toss or roll to coat the shrimp evenly.

Toss the blossom salad over the shrimp and finish with a sprinkle of walnut crumbs. Enjoy!

YIELD

Serves 1

SAUCE

2 tablespoons mayonnaise

1/2 teaspoon Amaretto

1 teaspoon honey

1/4 teaspoon fresh lemon juice

Pinch of ground cayenne pepper

BLOSSOM SALAD

3 edible flowers

Touch of lime juice

Touch of olive oil

1 teaspoon lime zest

Salt and pepper to taste

Sprinkle of walnut crumbs

SHRIMP

3 colossal shrimp (U10)

Cornstarch blend: 2 parts seasoned cornstarch (salt and pepper) and 1 part almond flour

1/2 cup light olive oil

3 cups butternut squash, peeled and medium-diced

1 cup celery, chopped

1 cup yellow onion, chopped

1 clove garlic

3 tablespoons canola oil

2 tablespoons pecans, lightly roasted

4 tablespoons pure maple syrup

4 cups vegetable broth or water

2 cups apple cider

Pinch of nutmeg

Salt and pepper to taste

Maple-Roasted Butternut Squash and Pecan Bisque

This is a seasonal favorite of many guests who call each fall to make sure that it will be on the menu.

Toss the squash, celery, onion, and garlic in the canola oil. Spread over a cookie pan and oven-roast for 45 minutes at 390 degrees (reduce roasting time by 20 minutes if using a convection oven).

Place the roasted ingredients in a soup pot and add the roasted pecans, maple syrup, broth or water, cider, and nutmeg. Bring to a boil and reduce to a simmer, skimming any froth off the top with a ladle.

Allow the soup to simmer gently for 30 minutes and remove from the heat.

Let the soup to cool, transfer to a blender, and blend to a smooth consistency.

Adjust the seasoning with salt and pepper, as desired, and enjoy hot.

YIELD

Serves 8

Corn and Zucchini Chowder

This delicious soup will taste better the next day once the flavors have been allowed to set. This is the Norwich Inn's most requested dish on cold winter nights.

Shuck the corn, save the cob.

Heat a thick-bottomed sauce pot to medium-high heat.

Add the oil, corn kernels, zucchini, potato, onion, celery, and bacon. Cook until the vegetables are translucent.

Add the chicken broth, thyme, and corn cobs and bring to a simmer. Simmer uncovered for 30 minutes.

Add the cream and bring to a simmer. Simmer for another 30 minutes.

Remove and discard the cobs.

Season to taste and serve.

YIELD
Serves 4

2 ears native corn

1 tablespoon olive oil

1 cup zucchini, small-diced

1/2 cup waxy potato (Yukon Gold), small-diced

1/2 cup onion, chopped

1/2 cup celery, chopped

1/4 cup maple-smoked bacon, finely chopped

3 cups chicken broth

1 sprig of thyme

1 cup heavy cream

Salt and pepper to taste

Rhode Island

AL FORNO
Providence

Providence, Rhode Island, is rich in history. First settled by Roger Williams in 1636, it was one of the original thirteen colonies. Williams, a refugee from religious persecution, got title to the land from the Narragansett natives. Williams had been a dissenter since he left the Massachusetts colony. Development of the Rhode Island colony was slow, purportedly due to the difficulty of farming the land, different and varying local traditions, and other factors.

During the 1770s, the British government stopped the progress of the industries of Providence due to high taxes that stifled the fishing, agricultural, and maritime industries. In fact the residents of Providence were the first to begin the bloodshed of the Revolutionary War during the Gaspee Affair in 1772. The Sugar Act had a devastating impact on Rhode Island distilleries, particularly the trade in rum.

The city of Providence actually escaped the tragedy of enemy occupation during the Revolutionary War; however, nearby Newport was captured. Brown's University Hall became a troop barracks and military hospital.

Following the war, the manufacturing sector became the focus, producing textiles, tools, and silverware as well as machinery. Gorham silverware was produced in Providence. At one time, the city claimed immigrants from Cape Verde, Portugal, England, Italy, Germany, Ireland, and Sweden. It was the ninth-largest city in the country and ratified a city charter in 1831.

During the Civil War, local politics split over slavery as many people had ties to Southern cotton. Despite ambivalence concerning the war, the number of military volunteers routinely exceeded quota, and the city's manufacturing proved invaluable to the Union. It is thought that the building used to be a stable for the city of Providence, and when George and Jo Al Forno were doing excavations on the building, they found troughs and stall dividers. It is thought that the building dates back to the 1800s.

The city was once nicknamed the "Beehive of Industry," while today the "Renaissance City" is a more common moniker, though, as of the 2000 census, its poverty rate was still among the ten

highest for cities with populations over one hundred thousand. No matter what the ups and downs of the history of Providence, one thing is for sure: as long as it claims Al Forno, it will be number one in the hearts of foodies.

Al Forno
577 S. Main Street
Providence, RI 02903
(401) 273-9760

2 cups heavy cream

1 cup canned tomatoes, chopped

3/4 cup Pecorino Romano,
    freshly grated

3/4 cup fontina, coarsely
    shredded

4 tablespoons Gorgonzola,
    crumbled

2 tablespoons fresh ricotta

2 small balls (4 ounces) of fresh
    mozzarella

1/2 teaspoon sea salt

2 cups fresh corn kernels, cooked

6 fresh basil leaves, chopped

1 pound dried conchiglie rigate
    or ridged pasta shells

4 tablespoons unsalted butter

Baked Pasta with Tomato, Cream, and Five Cheeses

Pasta in the Pink

Preheat oven to 500 degrees. Bring a large pot of water to a boil for the pasta.

In a mixing bowl, combine all the ingredients except the pasta and butter. Stir well to combine.

Generously salt the boiling water and drop in the pasta. Parboil for 5 minutes, stirring often. Drain the pasta (it will be too hard to eat; it cooks further in the oven) and add to the ingredients in the mixing bowl. Toss to combine. Divide the mixture among 6–8 individual small, shallow ceramic gratin dishes (1 1/2 to 2 cups capacity) for a first course or 4–6 individual medium gratin dishes for a main course. Dot with butter and bake until bubbly and brown on top, about 10 minutes.

YIELD

Serves 6–8 as a first course or 4–6 as a main course

Linguine with Clam "Bolognese"

Put the olive oil, onions, carrots, celery, garlic, and parsley in a large straight-sided sauté pan. Cook the vegetables over moderate heat until soft without browning, about 10 minutes.

Add the wine, raise the heat, and cook at a brisk boil until most of the wine has evaporated, about 3 minutes.

Add the clams, tomatoes, hot pepper, and a generous grinding of black pepper. Bring to a boil, reduce the heat, and simmer gently for 15 minutes.

Bring a large pot of water to a boil for the pasta. When the sauce is nearly finished, generously salt the pasta water and drop in the linguine. Cook at a rapid boil, stirring frequently, until al dente. Drain the pasta and add to the sauté pan. Toss with 4 tablespoons of the butter, or more to taste. The sauce should be glossy and clinging to the strands of linguine. Serve right away with the bread crumbs if you like.

YIELD

Serves 8 as a first course or 4–6 as a main course

1/4 cup extra virgin olive oil

1/3 cup onions, finely chopped

1/3 cup carrots, finely chopped

1/3 cup celery, finely chopped

2 teaspoons fresh garlic, finely minced

1 tablespoon flat-leaf parsley, finely chopped

1/2 cup dry white wine

1 cup clams with juice, finely minced

1 2/3 cups canned tomatoes, puréed

1 hot pepper, chopped or 1/4 teaspoon cayenne

Freshly ground black pepper

1 pound dried linguine

4–6 tablespoons unsalted butter at room temperature

Homemade sautéed or toasted bread crumbs (optional)

George's Toss and Tumble "Cheater's" Lasagna

2 tablespoons unsalted butter

5 cups fresh or prepared red sauce

1 batch fresh lasagna noodles

1 large ball (4 ounces) fresh mozzarella drained and cut into 1/2-inch slices

1 1/2 cups Parmigiano-Reggiano, freshly grated

1 cup ricotta

Bring a large pot of water to a boil and heat the oven to 425 degrees.

Smear some of the butter on the bottom and sides of a 10" × 14" baking pan. Cover the bottom of the pan with 1 cup sauce. Set aside. Put 2 cups sauce into a large mixing bowl. Set aside.

Generously salt the pasta water and cook half the lasagna noodles in batches. Drain and transfer the pasta to the mixing bowl with the sauce. Toss gently but thoroughly to ensure the sauce covers all surfaces of the noodles to prevent them from sticking together. Add half the mozzarella and half the Parmigiano-Reggiano. Toss together without making a homogeneous mix. Gently fold in the ricotta if you like, being careful to leave the mixture patchy. Tumble the whole thing into the baking pan without smoothing out the surface.

Repeat the process with the remaining sauce and the other half of the pasta, mozzarella, Parmigiano-Reggiano, and optional ricotta. Toss and tumble into the baking pan, purposely leaving high and low spots. Dot with the remaining butter and bake for 25 minutes, or until bubbling hot with portions of the top nicely browned. Cool for about 5 minutes and serve.

❧ YIELD ❧

Serves 8–10 as a first course or 6 as a main course

THE CHANLER
AT CLIFF WALK
Newport

The rich and famous all came to Newport, if not permanently, then at least for the summer. Many built their own residences. Congressman John Winthrop Chanler of New York City and his wife, the former Margaret Astor Ward, began construction of a Victorian mansion in 1870. It was completed in 1870 at a cost of $30,000, an astronomical sum at the time. They could afford it.

Mrs. Chanler was the niece of Mrs. Julia Ward Howe, author of "The Battle Hymn of the Republic" and the first president of the New England Woman Suffrage Association. She was also the niece of Mr. and Mrs. William Astor, one of the wealthiest families in America.

As you might expect, the mansion is steeped in history. It is the only hotel in Newport overlooking the Atlantic Ocean and the first mansion built on what is today the city's famous "Cliff Walk," also know as "Mansion Row." An article in the *Newport Mercury* dated January 4, 1873, refers to the Chanler mansion's location atop the cliffs as "one of the finest on the island" and adds that "the home is being built in an expensive manner."

The mansion has had many incarnations during its long history. In 1902, President Theodore Roosevelt visited when he became godfather of the owner's grandson. Originally called "Cliff Lawn," it was, for a brief time, a historical museum and at one time operated as the Tolethorpe-on-the-Cliffs Home and Day School for Girls.

More than eight centuries of history are reflected in the fourteen private rooms of the Chanler at Cliff Walk. Each room in the mansion's main building is decorated and named for a historic period. Various themes, such as twelfth-century Gothic and fifteenth-century English Tudor, are carried throughout each individual room with the use of furnishings, décor, antiques, and even bathroom fixtures that represent the particular era in order to give that room its own special personality and historical perspective. Some of the furnishings from the original Chanler Museum are incorporated into the rooms.

Although the mansion also had served as a boarding house and as a girl's school, it was not operated as a hotel until shortly after World War II, when it boasted thirty rooms. The hotel was sold at auction in 1956 for $40,000 and was renamed Cliff Walk Manner. The property was sold again in June 2000 to Detroit businessman John Shufelt, who renamed it the Chanler at Cliff Walk to focus attention

on the history of the original mansion, as well as its premier location. Shufelt closed the hotel to embark on an extensive renovation and refurbishing program. His wife, Jeanie, who oversaw the renovation, was also the artistic force in the remodeling of the nearby 147-year-old La Farge Perry House bed-and-breakfast, which Shufelt had purchased in 1996.

The Chanler at Cliff Walk embodies all the history of Newport, offering charm and elegance with a dramatic view of the Atlantic.

The Chanler at Cliff Walk
117 Memorial Boulevard
Newport, RI 02840
(401) 847-1300

Ahi Tuna Poke

Combine the tuna, avocado, cilantro, and chives into a mixing bowl. Pour the wasabi oil and ginger vinegar over everything and gently toss (careful not crush the avocados). Season with salt and pepper to taste. Serve in a lettuce cup.

YIELD

Serves 2

5 ounces fresh ahi tuna

1/4 whole ripe avocado, diced small

1 ounce chiffonade of cilantro

2 ounces chives, chopped, for garnish

1 tablespoon wasabi oil

2 tablespoons ginger vinegar

Salt and pepper to taste

2 lettuce cups

OCEAN VEGETABLE SLAW

1 cup fresh hearts of palm, julienned

8 ounces fresh sea beans (found at a specialty store)

4 ounces raw French beans, cut on a bias

1 cup prepared wakame seaweed salad (found at a specialty store)

4 ounces carrots, julienned

1/4 cup cilantro, chiffonade

3 ounces sesame oil

2 ounces wasabi oil

SOFT-SHELL CRABS

8 prime blue crabs, cleaned

1 3/4 cups all-purpose flour

3/4 cup corn starch

2 teaspoons sugar

2 tablespoons baking powder

Salt and pepper to taste

1 1/2 teaspoons sesame seeds, toasted

Pinch of togarashi

1 1/4 cups ice cold water

Crispy Soft-Shell Crabs with Ocean Vegetable Slaw

OCEAN VEGETABLE SLAW

Toss all vegetables in a bowl with sesame and wasabi oils. Reserve in refrigerator.

SOFT-SHELL CRABS

Prepare seasoned flour by mixing flour, corn starch, sugar, baking powder, sesame seeds, salt and pepper, and togarshi in a bowl. Chill. Dip each cleaned crab into the chilled seasoned flour. Shake off excess flour and cook crab at 350 degrees in a fryerator (deep fat fryer) until golden brown, one side at a time. If you do not have a deep fat fryer, you can use a sauté pan with 2 cups of canola oil. Flip the crab over to cook the other side only when the bottom side of the crab is crisp (you can check this by lifting it up to check.) Remove crab from the fryer and pat dry on a paper towel to remove excess grease.

PLATING

Season crabs with salt. Serve in a bowl with salad at the base of the bowl and two crabs placed on top.

YIELD

Serves 4

Roasted Pheasant Breast with Truffle-Scented Spaetzle and Parmesan

SPAETZLE

In a large bowl, combine eggs, egg yolks, and sour cream. Sprinkle flour in little by little, stirring the mixture continuously. Stir in salt, pepper, and nutmeg. Let dough rest for 15 minutes.

When ready, bring a large pot of salted water to a boil. Using a colander, press the spaetzle mixture through the holes of the colander into the boiling water. Little thick noodles will form and begin to float on the water. After 1 minute, strain and cool the spaetzle. Toss with a small amount of olive oil just to coat the spaetzle.

PHEASANT BREAST

Preheat oven to 300 degrees Fahrenheit. Season pheasant breast with salt and pepper.

Over high heat, add grape seed or canola oil to sauté pan and sear pheasant breast skin side down until crisp and golden brown. Flip the breast over and sear with the other side down for 30 seconds. Remove breast from the pan and place skin side down on an oven tray. Roast for approximately 6–8 minutes. Remove from oven and allow the pheasant to rest for 5 minutes uncovered.

SPAETZLE

2 1/2 each whole Grade A eggs

4 Grade A egg yolks

3 ounces sour cream

6 ounces flour

Salt and pepper to taste

Tiny pinch of nutmeg

1 teaspoon olive oil

PHEASANT BREAST

1 whole boneless pheasant breast

Salt and pepper to taste

2 ounces grape seed or canola oil

Truffle oil (found in a specialty store)

Shaved Parmesan cheese, for garnish

Chives, chopped, for garnish

Slice meat on a bias, cutting 4 equal portions. Arrange on a plate with the spaetzle. Serve with a drizzle of truffle oil, shaved Parmesan cheese, and chopped chives.

YIELD

Serves 2

THE HOTEL VIKING
Newport

Newport was growing quite rapidly early in the twentieth century. The local business establishment saw a great need for a grand hotel to keep pace with this economic growth. Fundraising began with the sale of common stock to the public. The issue sold out in a day, and construction began immediately.

The Hotel Viking opened to an awestruck public in May 1926. Separate parties were held for everyone who worked on the hotel and for the general public. Tickets for $5 were sold out for both functions. The American Hotels Corporation managed the property until the late 1960s.

The first motel unit was opened in 1962, with an outdoor pool and patio built in a beautiful landscaped setting. The name of the hotel was changed for a time to the Viking Hotel and Motor Inn. Guests could drive up to a modern two-way camera in the parking lot to check in. The second motel unit was added in the 1970s.

In 1964, the hotel added a thirty-thousand-square-foot convention center to the lower level, covering up the outdoor pool and surrounding area. This former convention center is now the Viking Ballroom, Spa Terre. In the 1980s, the new ownership connected the two freestanding motel units to the main building, making one large complex, and the hotel was renamed the Hotel Viking.

Noble House Hotels and Resorts became the new management company in 1999 when LaSalle Hotels bought the property. They have presided over several renovations since then. As a member of the prestigious Historic Hotels of America, the Hotel Viking holds a special place in history. The clock above the front desk depicts ancient Nordic runes, which are alphabetic script used by the peoples of northern Europe from the first century until well into the Middle Ages. The brass letter box in the lobby is a 1926 original.

The Hotel Viking offers a wonderful combination of style, comfort, and modern amenities. Brimming with stories of famous dignitaries and celebrities, the Hotel Viking has offered gracious

hospitality for over eighty years. The most recent renovations have restored the original guest rooms to their golden age.

The Hotel Viking
1 Bellevue Avenue
Newport, RI 02840
(401) 847-3300

Airline Breast of Chicken

"Airline breast" means that the drummette (the section of the wing that is connected to the body of the bird and contains most of the wing's meat) is still attached to the breast of the chicken. This was a popular way for commercial airlines to serve chicken because the breast retains more moisture. Thus, the chicken servings remained moist while they were kept in warming units onboard planes.

CHICKEN

Halve the chicken and then cut each half into two portions: one portion is the breast with the drummette or wing attached and the other portion is the leg with the thigh attached. A butcher at your specialty store or supermarket can do this apportioning for you.

Preheat the oven to 350 degrees.

Place the four chicken parts on a lightly oiled baking sheet or in a lightly oiled roasting pan and roast for 20 minutes, or until the internal temperature reads 160 degrees on a meat thermometer.

POTATOES

Boil the potatoes, remove the skin, and mash them with cream and butter. Render the pancetta in a saucepan over low heat and add to the mashed potatoes.

CHICKEN

1 whole chicken

1 tablespoon olive oil

Salt and freshly ground pepper to taste

POTATOES

1/4 pound Idaho potatoes

2 tablespoons heavy cream

1 tablespoon butter

1 teaspoon pancetta, chopped

280

BEANS AND MUSHROOMS

1/4 ounce fresh morel mushrooms (other mushrooms may be substituted)

1/2 ounce freshly prepared fava beans (other beans such as lima or soy [edamame] may be substituted)

1 tablespoon olive oil

CIDER SYRUP

1 cup cider vinegar

2 tablespoons brown sugar

1 teaspoon fresh thyme

BEANS AND MUSHROOMS

Sauté the fava beans and morel mushrooms in olive oil over medium heat until cooked through.

CIDER SYRUP

In a saucepan, combine the vinegar, brown sugar, and thyme and reduce the mixture to the consistency of a syrup.

PLATING

Spoon half the mashed potatoes into the center of a dinner plate, place the leg on top of the potatoes, and then stack the breast on top and drizzle with the cider syrup. Finish with the sautéed beans and mushrooms. Season to taste.

YIELD

Serves 2

Grilled Scallops with Napa Cabbage, Crispy Bacon, and Grain Mustard Cream

Chef Thiele uses sweet New England sea scallops in this dish and serves them with "bitter" Napa cabbage flavored with the taste and slight crunch of rendered bacon. Then he finishes this appetizer with the kick of grain mustard in a cream sauce—sweet, bitter, spicy, soft, and crunchy.

4 ounces bacon, finely diced

1 cup Napa cabbage, chopped

1/2 cup heavy cream

2 tablespoons grain mustard

Salt and pepper to taste

6 U8 sea scallops

In a small pan, render the bacon until crispy. Add the cabbage and sauté until it is thoroughly wilted and cooked through. Reserve.

In a small saucepan, add the cream, mustard, salt, and pepper to taste and reduce by half. Reserve.

In a grill pan, grill the scallops on both sides until cooked through, about 2 minutes per side.

PLATING

Spoon the cabbage in the middle of a small plate. Place three grilled scallops around the cabbage and finish with the mustard cream sauce.

YIELD

Serves 2 as an appetizer

 *282*

TUNA CEVICHE

1 shallot, minced

1/4 cup sugar

1/4 cup rice wine vinegar

Juice from 1/2 a lime

1 teaspoon red chili flakes

3 ounces yellow fin tuna, sliced
    very thin

SPICY CHUTNEY

1/2 teaspoon Thai chili, finely
    chopped

1/2 teaspoon jalapeño, finely
    chopped

2 teaspoons tomato paste

1 teaspoon curry paste

1 teaspoon cumin

1 teaspoon coriander

Tortilla chips, store bought or
    homemade

Tuna Ceviche with Spicy Chutney

Chef Thiele has put his own global spin on a traditional Peruvian ceviche by stacking the ceviche between crispy tortilla chips and topping the tuna with housemade spicy Indian chutney.

TUNA CEVICHE

In a small mixing bowl, combine the shallot, sugar, vinegar, lime juice, and red chili flakes. Whisk together. Add the tuna and chill for about 30 minutes.

SPICY CHUTNEY

Sauté the Thai chili and jalapeño in a small saucepan until soft. Slowly whisk in the tomato and curry pastes and add the cumin and coriander.

PLATING

Alternately stack the tuna between tortilla chips to create a three-layered appetizer, topping each layer of ceviche with a small amount of spicy chutney to taste.

YIELD

Serves 2 as an appetizer

PROVIDENCE BILTMORE

Providence

New York entrepreneurs John Bowman and Louis Wallick envisioned building a hotel to accent the age of the flappers. The Biltmore would be a state-of-the-art luxury hotel. It was designed by New York architects Warren & Wetmore, whose other commissions included Grand Central Station. The building's unique V-shaped design afforded all guests an outside room.

It was 1922, and F. Scott Fitzgerald spun tales of beautiful flappers and dashing aristocrats. Enthusiastic crowds danced to the hot licks of cool jazz musicians such as Louis Armstrong. Prohibition spawned secret speakeasies and backyard stills. Women were mesmerized by the images of Rudolph Valentino and Douglas Fairbanks on the silver screen. The discovery of King Tut's tomb brought everyone the awesome riches of ancient Egypt.

The opening of the Providence Biltmore Hotel in June 1922 epitomized this year of glitter and glamour. A front-page story in the *Providence Journal* reported on the banquet and ball that would officially open the Biltmore, forecasting that it would be "the most elaborate social event ever to be held in the city." More than one thousand people attended the party, including local officials and several prominent New York City hoteliers. For the occasion, the building was illuminated from top to bottom with more than twenty-five thousand lights.

The stunning six-hundred-room hotel included a drugstore, printing shop, carpentry and upholstery shop, and photo lab. The original Biltmore also featured rooftop gardens and chicken coops. Guests could choose from six different restaurants. Shortly after its opening, the local paper hailed it as the "new tourist and social center of Providence."

The hotel continued to be a local hot spot during the big band era of the 1930s and 1940s. The Garden Room resonated with the sounds of such famous orchestra leaders as Benny Goodman and Jimmy Dorsey. At one point, the dance floor was turned into an aquarium, complete with live fish, for a performance by Esther Williams. When Sonia Henie's ice show arrived, the floor was frozen solid.

This was also the era of the Biltmore's famous Bacchante Girls. Known everywhere for their beauty and poise, these were the waitresses in the trendy Bacchante Room. The dining area was very intimate, with dimmed lights and mirrored walls. Seating sections were called "banquettes,"

which were designed to hold between two and eight people. To be served, one simply pushed a button to summon a Bacchante Girl. She would appear in her costume, which featured a diaphanous skirt. The bar area had a glass floor underlit with pink lighting, a feature that advertised the girls' beautiful legs.

The stately Providence Biltmore has weathered the worst of the notorious New England weather. It has survived numerous hurricanes, including the famous storms of 1938 and 1954. The 1938 hurricane flooded the building to the point that water poured down the elevator shafts. Sofas floated through the Falstaff Room, drifted out into the lobby, and stopped just short of the revolving doors. A plaque on the lobby columns commemorates the high-water mark.

The hotel closed for a time from 1974 until 1979 and has undergone several renovations since then to restore its 1922 charm. The Providence Biltmore has been placed on the National Preservation Register as one of the country's cherished architectural treasures.

Providence Biltmore
11 Dorrance Street
Providence, RI 02903
(401) 421-0700

Providence Biltmore McCormick and Schmick's Grilled Swordfish

SWORDFISH

Coat the fish with vegetable oil and season with the salt and pepper. Grill over a very hot fire. The fish should be just barely cooked through. Place a 2 1/2-inch slice of sun-dried tomato butter on each steak.

SUN-DRIED TOMATO BUTTER

Combine all the ingredients and form into a log 1 1/2 inches in diameter. Wrap the butter in plastic wrap and chill or freeze.

YIELD

Serves 2

SWORDFISH

2 seven- to nine-ounce swordfish steaks

2 tablespoons vegetable oil

1/4 teaspoon salt

1/4 teaspoon pepper

SUN-DRIED TOMATO BUTTER

1/2 pound softened butter

4 tablespoons sun-dried tomatoes, chopped

2 tablespoons fresh basil, chopped

1/2 teaspoon red chilies, crushed

2 five- to six-ounce tilapia fillets

Flour to dust

2 eggs, beaten with 2 tablespoons milk

1 1/2 cups cashews, finely ground

1/2 cup Jamaican rum butter sauce (see page 287)

1/4 cup vegetable oil

1 tablespoon red pepper, finely chopped

1 tablespoon green pepper, finely minced

1 tablespoon yellow pepper, finely minced

2 tablespoons scallions, sliced to about 1/4 inch

Cashew - Crusted Tilapia

Bread the fillets by first dusting them with the flour, then dipping them in the beaten egg mixture, and finally coating them thoroughly with the ground cashews. It is best to do the breading an hour ahead of serving time, then allow the fish to rest in the refrigerator before cooking. While the fish is resting, make the Jamaican rum butter sauce and keep on the stove, but not over direct heat. (The sauce will break down if too hot.)

Heat the oil in a large sauté pan or skillet and pan-fry the tilapia. Cook the fish on both sides until golden brown, 3 minutes per side. Place the fish on serving plates and pour the sauce over them. Combine the red, green, and yellow peppers to make "pepper confetti" and sprinkle the dish with the scallions and peppers.

This dish is best when accompanied by rice and a simple grilled, sautéed, or steamed green vegetable like asparagus, spinach, or broccoli.

YIELD

Serves 2

Jamaican Rum Butter

Split the vanilla bean in half and place into a saucepan. Add both types of rum, the saffron, lime juice, pepper, and sugar. Remove the pan from the heat and stir in the butter to form into a sauce. Add a little butter at a time, allowing each piece to melt before adding more.

⮾ YIELD ⮿

About 1 1/2 cups

1/2 vanilla bean

1/4 cup white rum

1/4 cup dark rum

Pinch of saffron

1 tablespoon lime juice,
    freshly squeezed

1/4 habanero pepper, minced

1 tablespoon sugar

1/2 pound cold butter,
    cut in 1-inch pieces

RENAISSANCE PROVIDENCE HOTEL

Providence

❧ ———————————————————— ❧

The spread of the Freemason movement since its birth around the beginning of the seventeenth century produced a need for temples in which the local lodges could hold meetings. The lodge in Providence began building its own temple prior to the Great Depression, but the project had not been finished when the bottom fell out of the economy.

As the financial system went into a steep decline, so did the fortunes of the Masonic lodge members who were paying for the work. Ironically, it was the actual building masons who walked off the job when they were not paid. The Masonic temple (known locally as the "Mason Building") and an attached structure were abandoned at the beginning of the economic calamity. They remained unfinished for years though it was hoped that construction could be resumed.

When World War II began, the project was permanently halted. The unfinished buildings sat abandoned for years. In the 1950s, the adjoining structure was finally completed and opened as the Veterans Memorial Auditorium. The main building, which would have been the Masonic temple, remained abandoned until 2004.

Sage Hospitality Resources purchased this abandoned property and proceeded first to complete the construction and then to completely renovate the interior to provide Providence with a new luxury hotel. The Renaissance Providence Hotel opened in June 2007.

The building, constructed in the Greek Revival style, is located prominently on Francis Street opposite the Rhode Island State House. The nearby Providence Place Mall has made the site prime real estate. It is connected to the Veterans Memorial Auditorium next door by a small structure at ground level.

The Renaissance Providence Hotel has fully retained and meticulously restored the grandeur of this historic building, while the interior has been transformed into an elegant reflection of modern-day sophistication. A dramatic theaterlike lobby is a stage for associates to create memorable experiences for guests. "Performance artists" lead guests on a journey filled with delightful luxury. Free-spirited service, thought-provoking amenities, and imaginative twists serve as the backdrop for creating a stay that will inspire artistic expression, whatever it may be.

The hotel recently received a Green Certification from the Rhode Island Department of Environmental Management in honor of Earth Day. The certification recognizes the hotel for excellence in voluntarily abiding by green performance standards, implementing best management practices, and complying with environmental regulatory requirements.

The Renaissance Providence Hotel has taken extensive steps to be ecofriendly. The hotel installed energy-efficient windows and light fixtures, as well as water-conserving faucets. Only Green Seal–certified cleaning products are used, such as biodegradable detergents and cleaning supplies, and all guest room amenities comply with their standards.

The 272 guest rooms of this Marriott International hotel are housed behind the historic façade of the once incomplete Masonic temple. The $100 million historic restoration of the property is the most ambitious historic restoration in the history of Rhode Island. In recognition of the customs of the Masonic order, the street-level Temple Downtown Restaurant offers a loyalty program. Repeat guests earn loyalty points for future visits. In recognition of its status as a masterpiece of neoclassical architecture, the Renaissance Providence Hotel is listed on the National Register of Historic Places.

Renaissance Providence Hotel
5 Avenue of the Arts
Providence, RI 02903
(401) 919-5000

GRITS

4 cups milk

4 cups water

6 ounces butter

Salt and pepper to taste

2 cups stone-ground grits (such as
    Anson Mills brand)

SCALLOPS

4–8 large scallops, such as U10s

1/2 cup Portuguese chorizo or
    Andouille sausage, diced

2 teaspoons garlic, minced

2 teaspoons shallots, minced

2 tablespoons olive oil

2 tablespoons white balsamic
    vinegar or sweet cider
    vinegar

1/4 pound baby frisée, cleaned

Scallops and Grits

This can be served as an entrée or as an appetizer. Living in the South for twelve years, our chef grew to love grits. Not instant grits, but real stone-ground grits . . . the stuff that takes an hour to cook, not five minutes. You can't even compare the texture and flavor.

GRITS

Bring milk, water, butter, salt, and pepper to boil. Wisk in grits and keep stirring until liquid returns to a simmer. Simmer for approximately 45–60 minutes, or until grits are tender, stirring occasionally.

SCALLOPS

Sear scallops over medium-high heat until carmelized golden brown on each side.

Add diced sausage and render until cooked. Remove scallops and set aside.

Add garlic, shallots, and oil to pan and stir. Deglaze pan with vinegar and season to taste (this makes a warmed vinaigrette for the frisée).

PLATING

Put grits in a bowl and place scallops on top. Toss frisée in sausage vinaigrette and decoratively place on grits and scallops. Pour remaining vinaigrette on top.

YIELD

Serves 6

Rhode Island Salmon

This dish is very seasonal with the fresh chick peas and the corn, but you can replace the chick peas with any legume you choose and with corn that is available.

Season salmon liberally with salt and black pepper.

Render bacon until just beginning to crisp. Add corn, chick peas, garlic, and shallot and sauté.

Add thyme and deglaze with chicken stock. Cook until reduced to almost dry. Add tomato and swirl in cold butter. Season and hold warm.

Cook salmon to desired doneness on grill or in sauté pan.

Neatly form succotash on plate or in bowl and place salmon on top. Garnish with fresh thyme.

YIELD
Serves 3

2 six-ounce salmon fillets

Salt and pepper to taste

2 ounces apple-smoked bacon, diced

1 cup fresh corn off the cob

1 cup fresh Rhode Island chick peas (shucked and blanched until tender in salted water).

1 teaspoon garlic, minced

2 teaspoons shallot, diced

1 teaspoon fresh thyme, picked

1/2 cup chicken stock

1/4 cup tomato, diced

2 tablespoons unsalted butter

1 1/2 pounds tomatillos

5 garlic cloves

5 jalapeños

1 pound poblano chilies

1 pound Anaheim chilies

1 bunch of cilantro leaves,
    cleaned

4 pounds pork shoulder, trimmed
    of excess fat and cut into
    1-inch cubes

Olive oil

3 garlic cloves, minced

2 tablespoons fresh oregano

2 yellow onions

2 1/2 cups chicken stock or low-
    sodium chicken broth

Salt and pepper to taste

Bly's Chili Verde

This is great for entrée-sized portions served with grated cheddar or as an accompaniment to eggs, burritos, dips, and chips.

Clean and roast tomatillos and garlic cloves at 350 degrees for 15 minutes, or until browned.

Roast jalapeño, poblano, and Anaheim chilies over a gas flame or in a broiler until blackened all around. Place in a covered container to cool. When cooled, peel skins and remove seeds and stems.

Place all chilies, roasted garlic, and tomatillos into blender with cleaned and chopped cilantro and blend until smooth.

Season pork liberally with salt and black pepper. Brown pork in olive oil in batches in a large heavy-bottomed pot. Do not crowd pan to allow browning. Remove and set aside.

In the same skillet, add garlic, oregano, and large diced onion and cook until translucent. Add browned pork, blended ingredients, and chicken stock. Bring to a boil and then bring down to a simmer. Simmer uncovered, stirring occasionally, for approximately 2 hours, or until pork is tender. Salt to taste and serve.

Note: Any slow-cooked stew or soup will generally taste better the next day.

✎ YIELD ✎

Serves 6–8

VANDERBILT HOTEL AND RESIDENCE CLUB
Newport

Located on Aquidneck Island, Newport was founded in 1639 by men who had religious differences with the Puritans. The settlement soon grew to be the largest of the four original towns of Rhode Island, and many of the original colonists became Baptists.

Newport soon became the most important port in colonial Rhode Island. Religious tolerance there attracted a group of Jews who were fleeing the inquisition in Spain, establishing the second oldest Jewish congregation in America. Quakers also found refuge in Newport, and the Quaker meetinghouse is the oldest house of worship in the state.

Newport became a major center of pirate activity during the late seventeenth and early eighteenth centuries. So many pirates used Newport as a base of operations that the London Board of Trade made an official complaint to the English government. The most famous of these pirates, Thomas Tew, was so popular with the locals that almost the whole town came out to greet him after one of his voyages. In the 1720s, colonial leaders, under pressure from the British government, arrested and hung many pirates. They were buried on Goat Island.

Throughout the colonial period, Newport suffered from an imbalance of trade with the largest colonial ports. As a result, Newport merchants were forced to develop alternatives. For a time, Newport was the center of slave trading, and many fortunes were made at the slave auctions in the Old Brick Market. Farewell Street is the site of the Common Burial Ground, where most of the slaves were laid to rest.

In the fall of 1776, the British took over the city because it could be used as a naval base to attack New York. Most of Newport's population was pro-independence, and the ever-polite British allowed them to leave. Loyalists and British soldiers inhabited Newport for the next three years, and the Narragansett Bay area became one large battlefield, with Newport being a British fortress. In 1780, the French forces commanded by the Comte de Rochambeau landed in Newport and controlled the city for the rest of the war.

The war destroyed much of Newport's economic wealth, and most of the merchants departed. In the mid-nineteenth century, wealthy southern planters seeking to escape the heat began to build summer cottages in Newport. They attracted the attention of many wealthy families, including the Vanderbilts. The grand homes they built are now museums, schools, and hotels, with few families able to afford to use them privately. But the attraction has continued.

Both Presidents Dwight D. Eisenhower and John F. Kennedy used Newport as their "summer White House." John Kennedy and Jacqueline Bouvier were even married here in St. Mary's Church on September 12, 1953. Newport is not only the site of the last residence of Commodore Oliver Hazard Perry but also the home of the Naval War College. The U.S. Navy has also established a major training center here, along with the Naval Undersea Warfare Center.

Newport also served as one of two capitals of Rhode Island until 1900. This curious arrangement had the state legislature alternating sessions between Newport and Providence.

In 1908, at a ground-breaking ceremony, Alfred Gwynn Vanderbilt dedicated the Newport Men's Social Club to his father, Cornelius "Commodore" Vanderbilt, owner of the magnificent Breakers mansion and one of America's wealthiest men. The club symbolized the family's great admiration for Newport as it was a gift to the citizens of the city. Although Alfred perished aboard the *Lusitania* only a few years later, the club flourished for some time.

Doris Duke later bought the building as part of her restoration fund drive to revitalize the city. It has since been beautifully restored as the Vanderbilt Hotel and Residence Club. It offers distinctive luxury suites that are just steps away from the historic harbors, cobblestone streets, fine restaurants, and upscale boutiques that make Newport a unique New England resort destination.

"A woman is like a tea bag—only in hot water do you realize how strong she really is."

—Nancy Reagan

Vanderbilt Hotel and Residence Club
41 Mary Street
Newport, RI 02840
(401) 846-6200
(888) 826-4255

New England-Style Mac and Cheese

1 ounce fresh parsley

1 ounce fresh tarragon

2 ounces bread crumbs

Salt and pepper to taste

4 ounces assorted fish (whatever you like)

Oil or butter for sautéing

2 ounces onion, diced

1/2 clove garlic, minced

1 ounce of Pernod

1 cup heavy cream

5 ounces pasta, cooked

3 ounces smoked Vermont cheddar

Pecorino cheese (optional)

Shrimp (optional)

First, wash parsley and tarragon. In a food processor, grind parsley and tarragon while slowly adding bread crumbs until bread crumbs are homogenous, not overly dry, and consistently green throughout. Season with salt and pepper to taste.

Next, you can use any type of fish. Generally trim from other recipes and cut into 1/2-inch cubes. If you prefer a rarer fish, cut into larger cuts; cut smaller if you like your fish more well-done. Season lightly and place into a hot pan with oil or butter and add your diced onions and garlic. Sauté until a light sear appears on your fish and then deglaze with the Pernod. Add cream and begin to reduce the liquid quickly. Add the pasta. When sauce has reached the desired thickness, add your cheddar (you want the blocky texture of the cheese to stand out in your final dish presentation). Season lightly and remove from heat. Place the mixture into a low bowl or plate and dust the top of the dish with the green bread crumbs. Place in a broiler to brown the top. If you desire more cheese in this dish, grind chunks of pecorino cheese into the bread crumbs.

Serve hot and bubbly.

YIELD

Serves 2

Rhode Island Portuguese Little Neck Clams

Make sure that your clams have been scrubbed free of any dirt.

Add oil to pan and begin to heat slowly. Add chorizo, garlic, and onions. Begin to caramelize the garlic and onions slowly. Add peppers and sauté.

Next, deglaze the pan with a splash of white wine, about 2–3 ounces. Let the wine simmer for 1 minute before gently adding clams to the pan. Be careful not to drop them in; you may fracture the shells and create inedible small bits in the final product.

Add a pinch of freshly ground pepper and the tomatoes. Cover and reduce flame. While the clams pop open from the heat, the tomatoes will reduce to a more stewlike consistency. If this point is reached before the clams are open, add a 1/2 cup of water to further the steaming.

With a few minutes before serving time, add the basil and parsley and cover. Then, just before it hits the table, squeeze a bit of lemon juice over the mixture. You can adjust the salt and pepper, but be aware that most chorizo has quite a bit of salt added and may not need more.

30 little neck clams, cleaned

1 ounce of olive oil

6 ounces of chorizo, sliced into rounds

1 ounce of garlic, minced

4 ounces red onion, julienned

4 ounces of assorted fresh bell peppers, julienned (the more color, the more attractive)

2–3 ounces white wine

Pinch of freshly ground pepper

1 whole beefsteak tomato, cut into eighths

2 ounces fresh basil leaves, roughly chopped

2 ounces fresh parsley leaves, roughly chopped

Juice of 1/2 fresh lemon

Salt and pepper to taste

YIELD

Serves 2

RESTAURANT INDEX

RECIPE INDEX